Praise for *The Way of the SEAL* and Mark Divine

"*The Way of the SEAL* is a revelation. This book will transform you into a person for whom success—in all areas of life—is as natural as breathing. From small business owners to titans of finance, everyone can benefit from Mark Divine's brilliant insights."

—SUSAN SOLOVIC, AWARD-WINNING ENTREPRENEUR, MEDIA PERSONALITY, AND BESTSELLING AUTHOR OF *GIRLS' GUIDE TO POWER AND SUCCESS*

"Using his experiences as a martial artist, a United States Navy SEAL, businessman, and teacher/trainer, in *The Way of the SEAL,* Mark Divine delivers a set of tools and techniques that have been proven to develop a strong sense of purpose, a high level of mental toughness, and an ability to be more productive."

—ROBIN BROWN, CHIEF EXECUTIVE OF SCRIPPS GREEN HOSPITAL

"*The Way of the SEAL* is *The Book of Five Rings* for the twenty-first century. Mark Divine is a true master."

—DON MANN, FORMER U.S. NAVY SEAL AND AUTHOR OF *NEW YORK TIMES* BESTSELLER *INSIDE SEAL TEAM SIX*

"This is not just another business book; it's a combination of practical steps and insights from a man who understands the true meaning of leadership and personal excellence."

—CARMINE DI SIBIO, GLOBAL MANAGING PARTNER–CLIENT SERVICES AT EY

"Going into the 2012 Olympic Games, we were four cyclists who had only recently started training together for this event.... Mark Divine provided unique advice that helped us become a more tightly coordinated team."

—JENNIE REED, DOTSIE BAUSCH, SARAH HAMMER, AND LAUREN TAMAYO, 2012 U.S. WOMEN'S CYCLING TEAM, SILVER MEDALISTS

"*The Way of the SEAL* is a clear, actionable blueprint for personal success that contains the tactics and strategies to help you achieve your goals and become the person you want to be."

—HOWARD LOVE, FOUNDER OF LovetoKnow.com, SERIAL ENTREPRENEUR, AND VENTURE CAPITALIST

"Whether you are a Fortune 500 CEO, an entrepreneur building your own empire, a student, or an athlete, what you'll find in Commander Divine's book *The Way of the SEAL* is the complete roadmap for creating the next highest version of yourself. It's a must read!"

—JOE STUMPF, MASTER REAL ESTATE COACH AND FOUNDER OF BY REFERRAL ONLY

"Mark is more than a Navy SEAL, he has the ability to teach all of us how to be one in everyday life."

—JOE DE SENA, FOUNDER OF SPARTAN RACE

"Commander Mark Divine is a proven leader inside the elite U.S. Navy SEAL community and outside as a successful business owner and mentor to civilians. If you're ready to take a stand, and find purpose in your life, look no further than *The Way of the SEAL*."

—BRANDON WEBB, FORMER U.S. NAVY SEAL AND AUTHOR OF THE *NEW YORK TIMES* BESTSELLER *THE RED CIRCLE*

THE WAY OF THE

SEAL

Think Like an Elite Warrior
to Lead and Succeed

MARK DIVINE

Commander, U.S. Navy SEALs (Retired)

WITH **ALLYSON EDELHERTZ MACHATE**

Reader's
digest

The Reader's Digest Association, Inc.
New York, NY/Montreal

A READER'S DIGEST BOOK

Copyright © 2013 Mark Divine

All rights reserved. Unauthorized reproduction, in any manner, is prohibited.

Reader's Digest is a registered trademark of The Reader's Digest Association, Inc.

Library of Congress Cataloging-in-Publication Data
Divine, Mark.
  The way of the SEAL : think like an elite warrior to lead and succeed / by Mark
Divine ; with Allyson Edelhertz Machate. -- 1st Edition.
     pages cm
  ISBN 978-1-62145-109-9 (alk. paper) -- ISBN 978-1-62145-110-5 (epub)
  1. Leadership. 2. Strategic planning. 3. United States. Navy. SEALs. I. Title.
HD57.7.D594 2014
650.1--dc23
                                        2013035217

We are committed to both the quality of our products and the service we provide
to our customers. We value your comments, so please feel free to contact us.

                  The Reader's Digest Association, Inc.
                  Adult Trade Publishing
                  44 South Broadway
                  White Plains, NY 10601

For more Reader's Digest products and information, visit our website:
                  www.rd.com (in the United States)
                  www.readersdigest.ca (in Canada)

Printed in the United States of America

3 5 7 9 10 8 6 4

Acknowledgements

This book has been quite a journey, but it's just the first leg of a longer journey into an adventurous new world. Of course, I did not write this book alone—it represents ideas and insights I have gained over many years and from many mentors. My cowriter, Ally, prodded and poked me to make it better every step of the way, providing organization to my disparate thoughts and making this a much better book in the process. Thank you, Ally! My editor at Reader's Digest Books, Andrea Au Levitt, provided invaluable input into the structure and tone of the book, while Kevin Moran, my trustworthy agent, kept working to find a home for WOS long after I had moved on to other projects. Andrea and Kevin, thank you!

Let me acknowledge my first true mentor, Kaicho Tadashi Nakamura, founder of Seido Karate. Kaicho and his incredible tribe of students and teachers provided a solid foundation upon which I built my own mental toughness, emotional control, and spiritual strength. Thank you, Kaicho and the Seido team!

My yoga teacher, Tim Miller, deserves special mention as well. Tim is a legend in the yoga community and, lucky for me, lives in my hometown of Encinitas, California. Tim is the first American yoga instructor certified by Pattabhi Jois, the founder of modern Ashtanga yoga. Tim and Kaicho taught me that the training is "the way" and to walk my talk.

I greatly appreciate Ken Wilber for his contribution of integral theory to the world—WOS and Unbeatable Mind are influenced by his work. Other teachers, mentors, and friends I would like to thank include Tom Brown, from the Tracker School; Shane Phelps, of Saito Ninjutsu; Greg Glassman, founder of CrossFit; Robb Wolf, author of *The Paleo Solution*; Jerry Peterson, founder of SCARS; and authors

Seth Godin, Roy Williams, and Steven Pressfield, who have also inspired me through their writings.

In the SEAL Teams, I was fortunate to work with some of the most focused, intelligent, and intense warriors in the world. They guided my development as a SEAL, especially when I screwed up. The list includes, but is not limited to, Admirals McRaven, Harward, Metz, and Bonelli; Captains McTighe, Paluso, Wilson, and O'Connell; Commanders Zinke and Washabau; Master Chiefs Crampton, Laskey, Naschek, and Martin; as well as my other teammates at ST-3, SDVT-1, ST-17, NSWG-1, and SOCPAC.

I'm super grateful to my SEALFIT and CrossFit teams of coaches, supporters, and staff, including Lance Cummings, Glen Doherty, Chriss Smith, Dan Cerrillo, Brad McLeod, Charlie Moser, Shane Hiatt, Sean Lake, Dan Miller, Dave Castro, Rory McKernan, Greg Amundson, Tony Blauer, Erik Larson, Derek Price, Jeff Grant, Michael Ostrolenk, Stu Smith, Tommy Hackenbruk, Lindsey Valenzuela, Becca Voigt, Kati Hogan, Rich Vernetti, Cindy Chapman, Catherine Chapman, Melanie Sliwka, Dave Bork, Will Talbot, and John Wornham, for their loyalty, skill, and humor.

Thanks to Susie and Lees Divine (my mom and dad), who have been there for me and taught me so many different lessons throughout my life. I am eternally grateful for my wife, Sandy, who has been an amazing friend and supporter through my entrepreneurial roller-coaster ride. Also my buddy and son, Devon, who keeps me laughing and honest. Thanks, Sandy and Devon!

Finally, I am grateful beyond words for all my teammates and their families, who have sacrificed so much for this country. Hooyah!

—Mark Divine

Table of Contents

A Note to the Reader

I'm betting you're tired of the same old self-improvement and leadership information rehashed and repackaged again and again.

Perhaps you're an executive seeking new ideas on how to survive, or even thrive, in today's challenging economic and business environments. Maybe you're a student wondering what career to choose, how to have healthy adult relationships, and generally how to think and make better decisions. Or maybe you're a mom juggling a career, kids, and a husband, wondering how you can live up to your full potential when you feel pulled in so many directions. You could even be a Special Operations (Spec Ops) candidate looking to get an edge in order to improve your chances for qualifying.

Well, in all cases, you've picked up the right book at the right time. *The Way of the SEAL* is a new look at leadership and personal excellence—one forged in the deserts, jungles, burned-out cities, and oceans of the murky special operations world. I've taken my twenty years of experience as a Navy SEAL officer, flavored it with twenty-five years of martial arts and fifteen years of yoga training, and pulled lessons learned from six successful multimillion-dollar business ventures for a unique, highly effective, and accessible combination that anyone can use to become an elite operator.

No doubt you've read about the SEALs, or seen some rendition of their lives and missions in a movie or on the Discovery Channel. It's no revelation that SEALs are physical studs and smart, too. But consider this: The program graduates fewer than 200 new SEALs a year, total. This is out of thousands who try to make the cut. Over the last six years, would-be SEALs who've spent at least three weeks in my SEALFIT Academy programs have had more than a 90 percent success rate becoming bona fide frogmen. Why? Because I know how a SEAL thinks, acts, and trains. In this book, I intend to reveal these principles and practices and teach you to integrate them into your life so you can succeed at an elite level in all that you do. The U.S. Navy has spent enough of your tax dollars training my fellow special operators and me, so a little payback is in order.

People e-mail and call me all the time asking if only SEAL candidates can train with my company. The answer is a resounding "No!" In fact, though I launched our world-renowned Kokoro Camp program for SEAL and other Spec Ops candidates, more than 75 percent of attendees are business or other career professionals. I believe that though not everyone has the physical ability, opportunity, or even desire to become a Navy SEAL, anyone can develop the same mental toughness, leadership qualities, and winning attitude. If I could sell a bottled elixir that would give you the mind-set of a SEAL, I would. I haven't figured that out yet, so this book is the first shot across the bow.

I say with complete humility that I am uniquely qualified to write this book. Prior to my SEAL life, I was a CPA with an MBA from New York University's Leonard N. Stern School of Business. I may be the only CPA to become a SEAL—which really means nothing more than that I was utterly misplaced in my first career. Deciding at age twenty-five that I'd gone completely wrong with my life plan, choosing to quit everything so I could fulfill my desire to become a SEAL . . . saying it wasn't easy would be a ridiculous understatement. My parents had long expected me to join the family business (the Divine Brothers manufacturing company is over 120 years old). Shifting gears was a huge risk with a lot at stake for me both professionally and personally. I wish I'd had a toolkit like this to help me know myself and choose better goals when I first graduated high school at eighteen—I probably could've saved my family thousands of dollars and saved myself a lot of time and misery.

Through a special program for those without prior military experience or an ROTC background from school, the Navy ultimately selected me for Officer Candidate School and a spot at the renowned Basic Underwater Demolition SEAL Training (BUDS). I was honor man of my 1990 BUDS class, the top graduate out of only nineteen finishers from the 180 or so who "classed-up" with me. All told, I did nine years of active duty, then eleven as a Reserve SEAL Officer. The Navy mobilized and deployed me to the Middle East twice as a Reserve Officer, the last time in 2004 to Baghdad.

But as it turns out, business was in my blood after all.

After my first round of active duty, I founded a brewery restaurant, took the helm of a software company, and created an online support and training portal for Spec Ops candidates at NavySEALs.com. In 2006, after demobilizing from my last reserve stint, I formed U.S. Tactical, Inc., which the U.S. Navy Recruiting Command hired to set up a nationwide mentoring program for prospective SEAL candidates. This program succeeded in raising the pass rate on the candidate screening test from 33 percent to over 80 percent in the first year. In 2007, I decided to offer my training services to the public and started SEAL-FIT. Since then I have trained thousands with the principles outlined in this book, which are rooted in SEAL training and the disciplines of our predecessor warrior traditions, my exploration of somatic, mind-body practices such as yoga and karate, and my own experience with cross-discipline, whole-person training (what I call "integral training"). I've trained SEAL and other Spec Ops candidates, professionals of all types, and corporate executives. My laboratory is my renowned SEALFIT Academy, which forges mental toughness through challenging physical and mental training, and I've honed my techniques and philosophy through my latest venture, the Unbeatable Mind Academy, which teaches mental, emotional, and spiritual principles. Even I'm amazed at some of the transformations I've witnessed among my students.

Though we work in Teams, every Navy SEAL epitomizes the kind of leadership I'll teach you in this book. Like these elite warriors, a leader following the Way of the SEAL is a professional who first masters the power of his or her own thoughts, emotions, instincts, and unique abilities and in so doing gains the trust and respect of others, becoming a natural leader. Thus, the principles presented in this book build on the individual skills of the leader; this approach is essential, even if you don't feel you're currently in a leadership position at your job. Every elite operator has strong leadership skills, as crucial for leading oneself as for leading others. Though we've primarily focused on the business arena, these same skills will enable you to achieve top-level results in every aspect of your life.

What does it mean to undertake the Way of the SEAL?

- You will learn to simplify and clarify your life so you can drive forward with a strong sense of purpose, mission focus, and values that you live and not just think about. Your existence will feel meaningful and you will have no regrets.

- You will learn to remain calm and centered in the midst of the most serious storms you face in life.

- You will develop the mental toughness to dominate any task or challenge.

- You will cultivate your intuitive decision-making powers and sense danger and opportunity as they near.

- You will become more emotionally balanced, allowing you to understand where others are coming from so as to anticipate their needs.

- You will grow into a better leader who is more authentic, respected, trustworthy, and persuasive.

- You will become a better person, period. Your family, teams, and community will benefit from your strength and the world will be a better place for your contribution.

I am honored and humbled by your choice to embark on this journey with me. Embracing the Way of the SEAL is not an easy path—transformation doesn't come overnight, though you will start to notice changes in how you feel and respond to things as soon as you begin working with these principles. The key to extraordinary results is to replace old habits with new ones, including old ways of thinking, acting, and believing. If you can stick with me and integrate the WOS principles fully into your life, then you will achieve whatever goal you set your sights on, whether it's to get a promotion, launch a successful new business, attain a higher fitness level, enjoy a fulfilling home life and marriage, or earn an academic degree.

You will master simple techniques for dealing with change, functioning at high levels in chaotic situations and trusting your gut. You will make persistence a habit and learn to embrace risk, eliminating the crippling fear of failure. You will cultivate an "offensive mind-set" and deepen your awareness so that each decision you make is a powerful one-two knockout punch. You will learn to think unconventionally and know how to break the rules within the boundaries of ethical acceptance.

The journey of a thousand miles starts with a single step, and you have taken that step. Let's work together to cultivate the Way of the SEAL in your life, starting now. Hooyah!

—Mark Divine
Encinitas, California, 2013

LEAD FROM THE FIELD

You cannot travel within, and stand still without.
—JAMES ALLEN, BRITISH PHILOSOPHER AND AUTHOR (1864–1912)

It was September 1990. I stood with my classmates in front of 300 visitors, staff, and students at the Naval Special Warfare Training Center for our graduation ceremony, on the verge of becoming something most guys only dream of: a bona fide rootin'-tootin', parachutin', deep-diving, demo-jiving, running, gunning Navy SEAL frogman. Only months earlier I'd been in New York City, the perfect over-achieving conservative boy living the prototypical American dream. I had surrendered my childhood fantasy of battling evildoers and rescuing damsels in distress, blithely accepting the cultural push into the corporate channel where I racked up credentials and set my sights on a moneyed future. Society's drummer boy beat his drum, and I, like many of you, marched along oblivious to the much subtler drumbeat inside of me.

My path led me to accounting and consulting. Perhaps yours led you to medicine, law, banking, information technology, or any number of traditional fields. Some years later, you found yourself deeply entrenched in a career. Maybe you still love your work but wonder why success in your field has not also led to peace and happiness in other areas of your life. Or maybe one day you found yourself wondering how you got here, or worse, what you're doing here. Perhaps like me, you found yourself wondering why you aren't happy, and whether you've stepped onto the wrong boat in your life.

The proverbial straw that broke the camel's back came while I wrestled with the idea of leaving New York. I was unhappy with the daily grind, feeling more at peace during intense workout sessions at the dojo or running the early morning streets. During one of these runs, I noticed a poster for the SEALs outside a Navy recruitment office. "Be Someone Special," its alluring message read. "Yes!" I thought. "I want to be someone special. Right now, I feel like a cog in the wheel of a giant, cold machine." As I had in my childhood fantasies, I felt drawn to the idea of serving others, and excited when I imagined operating daily at the highest levels of performance and challenging myself on a team full of those who shared similar values. My decision was anything but clear, however, until I worked with my last client, Kane.

Kane & Co., a family-run paper company, had been caught up in the "influence-peddling scandal" of the Long Island defense industry in 1988. The company produced packaging used by defense contractors to ship large aerospace components. When the big contractors were exposed as having bribed government officials, smaller subcontractors like Kane got swept up in the investigation. The IRS focused on these easy targets and insisted they hire auditors to dig up and analyze their reams of data. My "Big Eight" consultancy assigned me, along with a supervisor and one other junior auditor, to perform the audit for Kane.

"These guys are never going to leave," I heard Joe Kane say through the office walls one afternoon. "They're gonna kill this business and Dad in the process." The founder's son was talking on the phone to his siblings, who were all desperately trying to keep the company afloat as Kane Sr. fought a sudden cancer brought on, the family believed, by the extreme stress of the audit. Sure enough, a month later Mr. Kane passed away.

The news hit me hard—I felt like I'd personally killed the guy. And Kane Jr. was right: We could've completed our work in three months, but our bosses kept sending us and billing the hours because they had the IRS behind them. The way we were bleeding this company horrified me. Kane was no longer the client; the primary motive became racking up billable hours.

The whole shebang looked like a pig with lipstick to me. How could I continue participating in this charade? I decided right then to commit to my fledgling purpose of becoming a warrior leader by serving in the Navy as a SEAL officer. I went back to the office and resigned immediately. I took a job as a personal trainer and doubled down on my karate and Zen meditation training, all in preparation for my SEAL bid. A month later, out of money and praying I had made the right decision, I received a surprise call from a partner at my former consultancy: "Mark, I'm starting a new firm, and I want you." I felt the familiar tug of my ego as I imagined the money rolling in. Then my inner voice said, "Stop!" and I remembered why I'd left my job in the first place. I knew with certainty I now traveled a better path, the right path for me. I politely turned the offer down.

One year later and here I was graduating from SEAL training, stepping into the next phase of my hero's journey, ready to accept whatever challenges lay in store. The presenter stopped speaking, and everyone turned to me as he extended the Honor Man plaque in my direction. One hundred and eighty candidates had started training six months earlier, and out of the mere nineteen who graduated, I finished at the top. I beamed as Captain Huth, Commanding Officer of BUDS (Basic Underwater Demolition SEAL training), pinned the coveted Trident—the gold insignia worn by a Navy SEAL—on my uniform.

The Trident marks you as someone special, a rare modern-day Spartan who trains harder, works smarter, and is courageous in the face of all challenges. To me, it also represents the Way of the SEAL, a mind-set and attitude that allows the wearer to be victorious on both the inner and outer fields of life's battles.

Let me teach you how you can earn your own Trident now.

What Is the Way of the SEAL?

As fast as the wind, as quiet as the forest, as daring as fire,
and immovable as the mountain.
—Battle standard of Takeda Shingen,
Japanese warrior (1521–1573)

I've been fortunate to study leadership as well as to observe it up close and personal from multiple perspectives. I've attended seminars and taught them myself at a major university. I have led and been led in large corporate and military settings, as well as in small businesses and on teams (a team being any group of people intentionally coming together to accomplish a mission or set of goals—this could mean a sports team, a volunteer committee, a department of employees, a married couple, or even a whole company or family). What I've noticed is this: Because there is no cultural emphasis on or education around embodying core values such as honor, courage, and commitment, aspiring leaders lack a foundation in their own character development, seeking career advancement without the means to become better people. As they adopt a particular model from a training event or book, they earnestly hope it will give them the ability to manage their leadership situations. They think, "All I have to do is apply the skills and act as the experts say, and things will be better." When their results fall short of the model's promise, these budding leaders lose faith and go looking for the next model.

Servant leadership, situational leadership, visionary leadership, gung-ho leadership . . . these are popular models, and they all treat leadership as a simple skill. But what if leadership is not a skill or a collection of behaviors? What if it's a character? We wonder why things don't work or continue to feel wrong when we spend so much time seeking the holy grail of leadership models instead of looking within, instead of building that character.

Bottom line: If you lack an underlying commitment to self-mastery and growth, even the best theory won't help you lead yourself or a team to success.

Embracing a New Approach to Leadership

One must ground authentic leadership in what I call an "integral development model," something I teach at SEALFIT through Five Mountain warrior training. The five mountains in my program represent the development of skills in the physical, mental, emotional, intuitional, and spiritual arenas; the integration of these skills thus results in a more balanced, whole-person growth. In *The Way of the SEAL,* we focus on primarily the mental, emotional, and intuitional. You will see, though, how this material can and should support your explorations in the other two arenas, and I encourage you to pursue them in a manner that suits your lifestyle and beliefs. The exploration of the physical mountain can vary so widely that it commands its own book (you can read about my recommended physical training program in my book *8 Weeks to SEALFIT*). The exploration of the spiritual mountain is inextricable from the other four mountains, so much so that you will naturally develop it to a large extent as you progress in the Way of the SEAL (a more focused spiritual development is a deeply personal journey, and again, extends beyond the scope of this book).

Strengthening in any one arena is relatively meaningless without the support of the others, like a table with uneven legs. You really need to develop all five simultaneously to tap into your potential and follow the Way of the SEAL. When you do, the result is a modern-day warrior in the ancient tradition, someone who achieves greatness with honor and humility, who naturally earns the respect of those whom he serves and leads.

I believe genuine leadership must stem from the heart of an individual, regardless of (and sometimes in spite of) the organizational role or power systems in which he or she is enshrined. Therefore, you'll find that the Way of the SEAL is predicated upon your commitment to fully develop personal discipline and an ethical stand; you'll focus on becoming a good teammate before stepping into the leadership arena. You will never seek leadership roles as an end in and of themselves. Ultimately, we need to develop what the Japanese call *kokoro*, which means to merge our heart and mind in action. It implies that we are balanced and centered, allowing us to operate in synchronicity with our inner selves, with others, and with nature. When we commit to integral development and lead with kokoro, we will be 100 percent authentic, present, and powerful.

The world needs leaders who will lead from the front and push from the rear; who will stand up and step out, risking more to enforce integrity at all levels—self, team, and organization—in what I call a "three sphere" approach. Combined with the other skills, tactics, and strategies in this book, this unique conceptual tool will greatly improve your chances of winning ethically and sustainably in today's fast and complex business climate. And a multidimensional perspective will never fail to give you an edge against those with a more narrow or nearsighted approach. We also need organizations to embrace this concept and support the development of individuals and teams by allowing risk and failure in order to foster true learning—the kind that develops the deep character that authentic leadership requires.

This sea change in thought and behavior won't happen because of any one book, course, or event. It will come about only through developing one authentic leader at a time. It starts with you and your commitment to personal excellence. As you follow the Way of the SEAL, you not only create a better you, but you also help create a better world.

Ancient Values for Modern Times

To think and act like a Navy SEAL is to pursue integral development and whole-person growth within a warrior context. Though this has an inherently militaristic flavor, I consider the term "warrior" to have a broader, more figurative meaning as one who is committed to mastering himself or herself at all levels, who develops the courage to step up and do the right thing, all while serving his or her family, team, community, and, ultimately, humanity at large. To achieve SEAL-worthy success, you must:

- establish your set point, turning a deep sense of values and purpose into a touchstone that will keep your feet in the sand and your eyes on the goal
- develop front-sight focus so nothing can derail you on your way to victory
- bulletproof your mission to inoculate your efforts against failure
- do today what others won't so you can achieve tomorrow what others can't
- get mentally and emotionally tough, and eliminate the "quit" option from your subconscious
- break things and remake them, improving them through innovation and adaptation
- build your intuition to utilize the full range of your innate wisdom and intelligence
- think offense, all the time, to surprise your competition and dominate the field
- train for life to develop mastery of your physical, mental, emotional, intuitional, and spiritual selves

Though many of the techniques and practices in this book are unique, the essence of these principles isn't new or trendy. In fact, a close study of ancient warriors such as the Spartans, Apache scouts, and samurai—bands of elite operators who are predecessors to the SEALs and other Spec Ops teams—reveals similar behaviors and philosophies. These cultures embodied a different set of values from what has become the norm in modern society. Today's Western culture is narcissistic. Our economic mythos—the collective story we tell ourselves about how our economy works and how we should interact as part of it—is based upon an individual carving out his or her slice of a limited-resource pie in a competitive attempt to secure a declining standard of living. The financial meltdown of 2008 and the long recession that followed forced many into undignified jobs; onto the dole; or to flat-out begging, borrowing, or even stealing. In all sectors, the norms of behavior have gotten very loose, with personal values around earning a living (and many other things) growing slippery.

Our daily crush of commitments keeps the hamster wheel of survival spinning, but it masks a growing unease and keeps attention off what matters most. It also obscures the grim reality that we are still responsible for our thoughts and actions, and the universe ultimately holds us responsible as well. We all pay at a personal and societal level for the failure to hold ourselves accountable to higher standards.

The Way of the SEAL is not a quick fix. It's a journey, a way of being. Yes, I'll give you strategies and tactics you can employ right away. In the end, however, the key factor is your own development into someone who can live these values and principles, and not just speak them. The journey starts with this book and continues as you practice the principles I'll lay out for you, finally stepping into the field to risk failure and judgment, but ultimately achieving the most profound and sustainable growth.

How to Use This Book

> Those who dream by night in the dusty recesses of their minds wake in the day to find that it was vanity: but the dreamers of the day are dangerous men, for they may act their dream with open eyes, to make it possible.
> —T.E. LAWRENCE A.K.A. LAWRENCE OF ARABIA (1888–1935)

If you work through this book thoughtfully and with dedication, the fruits of your labor will start showing immediately. Mastery, however, will take a lifetime. I encourage you to enjoy the journey and victories as they come your way. You'll notice that as you learn and grow, the victories will accelerate. So will the size and number of challenges. As a follower of the Way, you won't shy from these; instead, you'll embrace them as the opportunities they truly are. For this, you'll need to develop focus, discipline, patience, and humility (and this book will help you do so). You will become a person of honor in the process. You will become an authentic leader of both yourself and others. You will earn your personal WOS Trident every day.

Throughout this book, you'll hear enlightening examples from my SEAL days and my personal journey in the business world, as well as powerful stories from my students and famous entrepreneurs. Each chapter represents one of the eight principles of living the Way of the SEAL and contains a close look at the core tenets or concepts you must learn. Some may seem familiar, while others will be new to you. All, however, play a role in the daily life of a WOS leader and will propel you through incredible transformations and toward the success for which you've been searching. I live these principles, my students live them, and now you will benefit from them as well.

I've structured the material to introduce you to the principles first; short drills throughout and robust exercises at the end of each section will help make the principles concrete for you and are an essential part of your training. As we go along, we'll sometimes circle back and go deeper into the techniques and skills for a more robust understanding and a more powerful application. Keep in mind that this material takes time to integrate into your life and being. I share these principles and techniques with my Unbeatable Mind Academy students over the course of twelve monthly lessons and in an intense immersion learning experience through my three-week SEALFIT Academy. I recommend you read the book once through, then go back and work with each principle as a monthlong exercise.

The irony is that we don't learn leadership from books or seminars—that is, until we embody the lessons through experience. You can't follow the Way from behind your desk or by maintaining the status quo. It isn't enough to simply read this book, though it will introduce you to important new ways of processing your experiences.

You have to put the principles to work—do the exercises, meditate on the ideas, talk about them with your team. The final chapter, "Training in the Way of the SEAL," brings it all together and shows you how to develop a personalized training plan. You must earn your leadership stripes in the field, not in the classroom.

Speaking of which, there will be mentors to guide you along the way. As they say, when the student is ready, the teacher will appear. My journey brought me into contact with Seido Karate Grandmaster Nakamura first, and then with many selfless mentors on the SEAL Teams and a few more since. I had to learn my way to the doorstep of each of my mentors, as will you with yours. However, the first step in following the Way of the SEAL isn't to search for a mentor; you start by searching for yourself. So let's bring it back to square one with some fundamentals.

ESTABLISH YOUR SET POINT

The hardest challenge is to be yourself in a world where
everyone is trying to make you be somebody else.
—E. E. CUMMINGS, POET (1894–1962)

More than seven billion souls on planet Earth and not one of us is the same. What really makes us different is not our skin color, language, or body, but our inner sense of who we are. Some may call this inner sense the soul or spirit. Whatever you call it, right now it has a set point, a fixed point on your internal reality map that will help you navigate when the path forward isn't clear or when challenges arise. It's that inner drumbeat, that voice whispering to you in important moments. You're probably thinking right now, "Do I have a set point?" If not, are you ready to discover it and begin to live your authentic life?

Establishing your set point requires you to:

- make a stand
- find your purpose
- embrace risk, loss, and failure

If you don't establish your set point, and don't connect every action to it so you can answer, "Why am I doing this?" in the face of great personal risk, then you can easily be derailed by circumstances or other people's desires for you. The perpetual winds of pleasure blow you in one direction. The gusts of pain push you in another. The problem is this keeps you from living your ideal life. You're simply bouncing around. By defining your stand and purpose, you will be able to use them as an internal GPS. When the winds of pain and pleasure blow, you won't change course.

Make a Stand

Unless we stand for something, we shall fall for anything.
—REV. PETER MARSHALL, U.S. SENATE CHAPLAIN
(1902–1949)

Toward the end of my program at Officer Candidate School (OCS), the commander left the field to come in and meet with me for the delayed SEAL officer candidate interview. In his office, the six-foot-two-inch, swarthy, uberfit SEAL commander sat on the edge of a table staring intently at me. Ten minutes passed without a word. As I sat there trying not to fidget, I remembered the staring contests I used to have in Lake Placid with my brother Brad. Every kid does that, right? Little did I know I was forging a crucial skill for gaining entrée to a band of elite warriors. The "thousand-mile stare" is a noteworthy trait of a SEAL, and you can be sure that Commander Woody was the poster boy.

Understanding slowly dawned on me. How I demonstrated control in even a subtle test like this would be a key to my character. Could I withstand the brutal hammering at BUDS? Would I deteriorate in the withering jungles of Southeast Asia or the frigid tundra of the Arctic? Could I be broken in an interrogation? "What does he see?" I wondered as I stared back as calmly as possible. Suddenly, his voice broke the silence, startling me.

"What do you stand for, Mark?" he asked.

Whew! Finally. "Ah, well, I stand for justice, integrity, and leadership," I said.

"I didn't ask for your vanilla values, son! What are your rock-bottom beliefs, that stand beyond which you won't be pushed? Don't just tell me what your family or society thinks you should believe in."

I guess my cheerful, somewhat cocky attitude (which I often mistook for confidence as a young man) didn't impress him. So I took a moment and reflected more deeply. I thought about my upbringing, all the competitive sports I'd played, my education, even the long treks I took with my father in the Adirondacks. What did these experiences teach me to stand for? I wasn't sure. A stand, I suspected, was your character speaking. So what was my character? I thought back to the schoolhouse of real learning I had attended over the last four years—the Seido Karate dojo—and realized my evolving worldview and ethos was most influenced by the warrior principles I was introduced to under Grandmaster Nakamura's watchful eye.

One weekend at the Zen Mountain Monastery in Woodstock, New York, after an hour of meditation and two hours of physical training, Grandmaster Nakamura gave us a short lecture that came back to me during the OCS interview. "When you bring your full attention to each moment, a day is a complete lifetime of living and learning," he said. "And we are not just training our bodies. You must prepare your mind, body, and spirit. Sure, it's easy to train here or there, to remove stiffness and improve fitness. But what about your kokoro, your spirit? Through your training, you work hard to remove stiffness of that also. That is what we do, day in and day out. In this way, your destiny is in your control."

Remembering this, I found my voice and said to the commander, "Destiny favors the prepared in mind, body, and spirit."

"Okay!" he said, his stern expression warming up a bit. "Now we're getting somewhere. What else?"

I kept talking, searching my inner space for my "lines in the sand." It was a difficult task. Later that evening, I reflected on this fateful conversation and wrote the following personal stand:

- Destiny will favor me if I am prepared in mind, body, and spirit.

- There's no free lunch; I must work harder than expected and be more patient than others.

- Leadership is a privilege, not a right, and I must earn it in the arena of action.

- As a warrior, I will be the last to pick up the sword but will fight to protect myself, my family, my country, and my way of life.

- I will strive to live in the present, resolve with the past, and create my ideal future.

- I will find my peace and happiness through seeking truth, wisdom, and love, and not by chasing thrills, wealth, titles, or fame.

- I will seek to improve myself, my team, and the world every day.

Most of us don't take the time to think deeply about our personal ethos. I didn't, until forced to by the good commander. However, once I was able to articulate it, the stand became a very real and powerful guiding force. When faced with murky and difficult decisions, I would fall back to my stand and see where a potential choice placed me. If it placed me outside my stand, then I wouldn't do it. A good example of this was my decision to leave the active-duty Navy.

Immediately after my marriage in December 1994, the Navy deployed me to SEAL Delivery Vehicle Team ONE in Hawaii. My newly minted wife, Sandy, came with me, of course, and we settled in. The higher-ups insisted there were no plans to send me overseas for "a while," yet two weeks later I got orders to Korea. Sandy found herself completely alone—we'd barely been in Hawaii long enough to make friends. Finally, after two months, I returned to her. Again the Navy told me I wouldn't be sent away for a while, but after a two-week break, they shipped me off to California for a six-week mission.

When I came back this time, I saw the writing on the wall. "I can't do this," Sandy confessed. "I knew you'd be away sometimes, but this is just too much. If this is how our life will be, I don't think we're going to work." We loved each other, but it was clear that regardless of what promises I made, the Navy's needs would always come first and would have me gone ten months out of the year. The old saying, "If the Navy wanted you to have a wife, they woulda issued you one!" suddenly sounded true. After six and a half years, I still loved the SEALs . . . the adventure, the missions, my teammates. I also loved my wife, and I wanted to build a family. It was an extremely difficult decision, but my stand was my guide, in particular this statement: "I will strive to live in the present, resolve with the past, and create my ideal future." So I chose to leave active service in 1996 for the Reserve Force and for my marriage. After twenty wonderful years with Sandy, fourteen of which have included our son, Devon, I can say with conviction that it was the right choice.

Developing a "stand" builds a foundation that supports our day-to-day activities and helps us move toward our purpose in life. Your stand answers the question, "What would I do?" as in, what would you do if you observed a major breach of integrity in your organization? If your teammate needed help; if you screwed up and the blame fell on someone else; if your country, community, or family needed you, what would you do? Your stand is the articulation of your character, which guides your behavior.

A great example is the SEAL Ethos, which serves as an insightful glimpse into the mind-set of an elite warrior. The SEAL Teams originally passed this incredibly strong stand down through their culture and legends. As time wore on (the SEALs as we know them today formed out of the fabled Underwater Demolition Teams in 1963), SEAL leaders realized they should codify and write down their ethos in order to guide future generations of frogmen. Thus, in 2006, sixteen years after I joined the force, the document now known as the SEAL Ethos came into being (see sidebar on page 16). Though the SEAL Ethos is a team ethos, the power it holds makes it a great guide for one's personal stand as well, and I have since adopted elements of it for my own. The *Reader's Digest* version is:

- maintain loyalty to country, team, and teammate
- serve with honor on and off the battlefield
- be ready to lead and ready to follow, and never quit
- take responsibility for your actions and the actions of your teammates
- excel as warriors through discipline and innovation
- train for war, fight to win, and defeat our nation's enemies
- earn your Trident every day

Leading from the field requires that we first know ourselves, our true nature, inside and out. When we live in full awareness of our stand, then we can face fear with courage. Fear is natural, something to be faced and understood, not to be avoided. Finding the courage to act in the presence of fear is the Way of the SEAL.

United States Navy SEAL Ethos

This is the stand that every SEAL learns:

In times of war or uncertainty, there is a special breed of warrior ready to answer our Nation's call. A common man with uncommon desire to succeed. Forged by adversity, he stands alongside America's finest special operations forces to serve his country, the American people, and protect their way of life. I am that man.

My Trident is a symbol of honor and heritage. Bestowed upon me by the heroes that have gone before, it embodies the trust of those I have sworn to protect. By wearing the Trident, I accept the responsibility of my chosen profession and way of life. It is a privilege that I must earn every day. My loyalty to Country and Team is beyond reproach. I humbly serve as a guardian to my fellow Americans always ready to defend those who are unable to defend themselves. I do not advertise the nature of my work, nor seek recognition for my actions. I voluntarily accept the inherent hazards of my profession, placing the welfare and security of others before my own. I serve with honor on and off the battlefield. The ability to control my emotions and my actions, regardless of circumstance, sets me apart from other men. Uncompromising integrity is my standard. My character and honor are steadfast. My word is my bond.

We expect to lead and be led. In the absence of orders I will take charge, lead my teammates, and accomplish the mission. I lead by example in all situations. I will never quit. I persevere and thrive on adversity. My Nation expects me to be physically harder and mentally stronger than my enemies. If knocked down, I will get back up, every time. I will draw on every remaining ounce of strength to protect my teammates and to accomplish our mission. I am never out of the fight.

We demand discipline. We expect innovation. The lives of my teammates and the success of our mission depend on me—my technical skill, tactical proficiency, and attention to detail. My training is never complete. We train for war and fight to win. I stand ready to bring the full spectrum of combat power to bear in order to achieve my mission and the goals established by my country. The execution of my duties will be swift and violent when required yet guided by the very principles that I serve to defend. Brave men have fought and died building the proud tradition and feared reputation that I am bound to uphold. In the worst of conditions, the legacy of my teammates steadies my resolve and silently guides my every deed. I will not fail.

Find Your Purpose

Know Thyself.

—ANCIENT GREEK PROVERB, FOUND AT THE GATES
OF THE ORACLE OF DELPHI

The last statement I made to Commander Woody during my interview was, "I believe that we all have a God-given purpose, and we won't be fulfilled unless we're living that purpose in a meaningful way."

"And what is your purpose?" he asked.

"To be a warrior and a leader. To master myself so I can fulfill this purpose as best I can."

I'd been aware of this driving purpose in my life since I first saw that SEAL recruitment poster, but it never felt clearer to me than in that moment, bolstered by expressing my stand. The difference between a purpose and stand is distinct: Our stand is a core set of beliefs. For instance, I left my CPA firm after the Kane episode because I couldn't work for an organization with such a singular focus on money at the expense of others' well-being. Having that stand helped me clarify my purpose: I felt the SEALs would represent the opposite end of the value spectrum from my financial career, emphasizing integrity, being honorable and authentic as a leader, and functioning within an interdependent community of trust while accomplishing inspiring and important things.

Your stand will answer the question "What would I do?" and your purpose will answer the question "Why am I here?" This weighty question presupposes that you have a unique reason for existing and a unique offering for the world. My experience is that everyone does, though we must look deep within to find it.

What's Your "Why"?

My first day of SEAL training found me in a two-hour beach beatdown session so brutal the helmets of quitters had already started lining up. But the sun was shining; we were on the beach in Coronado, California, being paid to work out. Life seemed pretty good to me, in spite of the momentary discomfort. Unfortunately, my buddy Bush didn't agree. Even though he'd been completely gung-ho throughout Officer Candidate School and could outrun and outtrain me most days, he turned to me as we did reps in the sand and said, "Mark, I can't do this."

I shouted over the din, "Bush, we just started . . . shut up and get through this." It seemed to work for a few minutes. Then Lieutenant Zinke, the First Phase Training Officer, ordered us to hit the surf. We jumped up and ran toward the water's edge. Bush ran the other way and rang the bell, ending his bid to be a SEAL.

Later when I asked him what happened, he shrugged and said sheepishly, "Ah, well. I actually wanted to be a veterinarian anyway." He didn't seem too upset, but I was dumbfounded. Bush spent several years thinking and telling everyone he wanted to be a SEAL. He went through all the motions, training his body daily and working his butt off to receive one of only a few slots for officers. However, in that crucial moment of pain and challenge, he quit.

During my Kokoro Camp program, I ask my trainees, "What is your 'why'?" I listen carefully, because their motivations are often a clue to who will make it and who won't. One guy, a SEAL candidate, says, "To prove to my father that I have the right stuff." Fail. That's an extrinsic motivator—i.e., powered by someone else's values—and thus not powerful enough to provide drive in the tough spots. Another says, "To be a better man so I can also be a better father." This guy, a 40-year-old gym owner, shows definite promise with a strong intrinsic motivation, one arising from his heart and deepest personal values.

It's no coincidence that an early challenge at Kokoro Camp is a famous CrossFit Hero workout we call "Murph" in honor of my SEAL teammate Lieutenant Michael Murphy. During Operation Redwing in Afghanistan, a shepherd and his son accidentally compromised the location of Murph's four-man sniper-observer team. Shortly thereafter, a mob of fighters overtook the SEALs. Murph's team valiantly fought their way down a rugged mountaintop, taking hits. Ignoring his own safety, Murph stepped into the open to use his satellite phone, the only place he could get an uplink. As he connected and relayed the position to his backup force, the fighters mortally wounded Murph.

In that instant of choice on the mountaintop, just as the SEAL Ethos promises, Murph did not quit. As the officer in charge, he knew his purpose was to lead his team through the mission to success and then bring them back home safely as a microcosm of his greater purpose of protecting and serving his country. He was able to answer the question "Why?" with confidence and do the right thing, even though it cost him everything.

So, what was the difference between my buddy Bush and Lieutenant Murphy? In the clutch, Bush couldn't answer the question

"Why?" He had no stand to keep his feet in the sand that day, no set point, no meaning to hold on to through the pain. Murph, on the other hand, intimately knew his purpose as a SEAL, and in his time of crisis, he instinctively relied on his stand, which provided detailed instructions to guide his behavior. If Bush had had a similarly clear purpose, and if he'd had an articulated stand grounding him that perhaps included a commitment to growth through hard work and to seeing things through, he would have had something to keep him putting one foot in front of the other.

Let's face it, when the stakes include your own mortality, you tend to get very clear about what's important. Bush was not facing mortal consequences, nor had he considered the question "What would I do if this decision were my last?" He lacked clarity on the important things in his life. Though an extreme example, Murph's story illustrates the power of knowing your stand and purpose and using these as your set point. If being true to your purpose and stand gets you killed (or fired, or dumped, or whatever), then it's an honorable death, and that's the point. True warriors accept that. Of course, it's highly unlikely that the fatal level of choice Murph faced will ever apply to you, but imagine the possibilities when you develop clarity at the level where each choice has life-or-death consequences. Living with this level of insight fuels every decision you make for the rest of your days, leading to a powerful new experience where you will do everything to create the life you were meant to live.

Embrace Risk, Loss, and Failure

Only those who dare to fail greatly can ever achieve greatly.
—ROBERT F. KENNEDY, U.S. SENATOR AND
ATTORNEY GENERAL (1925–1968)

One final comment before we dive into the rest of this book: I understand that risking loss and failure isn't easy. I certainly struggled with it while contemplating leaving the high-paying corporate world for service in the military. This single decision ensured that financial freedom, which I valued highly at the time, would be improbable. My decision-making process also suffered the burden of knowing my family's pain and disappointment with my career shift, the potential for failure in my quest to become a SEAL . . . not to mention the possibility of death in training or combat! Did I feel intimidated and scared sometimes? Hell, yes! However, despite all this, deep inside I knew I was on the right path. The universe has since rewarded me many times over for that courage. And, yes, my family got over it and my mom still loves me.

As we begin our journey in the Way, doors will start opening, and a breeze of opportunity, tinged with pleasure, pain, or maybe both, will blow in. We can choose to ignore the open doors or walk on through. Walking through is the more rewarding option. Heed this well and you will soon earn your own WOS Trident.

★ ★ ★ EXERCISES ★ ★ ★

THE WAY OF THE SEAL (WOS) ASSESSMENT

This multipart exercise begins the journey of self-discovery. This intensely personal process begins with a relaxation and contemplation exercise. As you ponder these questions, pay close attention to any images and feelings that arise—these raw initial impressions come from your subconscious mind, as yet unfiltered, unanalyzed, and uncategorized. These are the clearest signs pointing to your purpose. Try not to judge what comes up, even (or especially!) if the message seems scary.

You will begin with the stand, because this is your rock-bottom belief system. Then you will define your values, which will further guide your behavior by encouraging or discouraging certain actions. Next, you will explore those things you are most passionate about, because these fuel your purpose and are where you should be directing more energy in the future. Last, you will uncover your purpose. Often your driving purpose is at odds with your current reality—that's why you need to unearth it.

Part 1: Build Your Stand

Your stand answers the question "What would I do?" First, find a comfortable place to sit with your journal, perhaps a chair or on the floor with your back against a wall. Make sure your spine is straight. Close your eyes and breathe with deep abdominal breaths for at least five minutes. While breathing, just relax deeply. This practice will ground you, settle your mind, and connect you with your subconscious. You'll be more sensitive to imagery and feelings in this state.

After at least five minutes of deep breathing, open your eyes and contemplate the questions below. Write your answers quickly, paying attention to the images and feelings that come up.

- What would I do if I knew I only had one year to live?
- What would I do if a natural disaster or terrorist event struck my town?
- What would I do if a friend asked me to help him move but I really wanted to go see a movie that night?
- What would I do if I found out my favorite brand had been exploiting workers and participating in environmentally destructive practices?
- What would I do if I won the lottery?
- What would I do if someone decided to fight me for no good reason?
- What would I do if an opportunity for an inside deal came my way with no chance of anyone finding out?
- What would I do if my team were bashing a teammate behind his back in my presence?

Now think about what your answers say about your character. For instance, my answer to the last question is "I'd keep my mouth shut and leave, if possible." For my stand, this translates into "I respect people's right to have an opinion, but I will not engage in negative talk or gossip." What if your friend asks you to help him move and you answer, "Sorry, but I have plans"? That could indicate you are operating out of selfish needs rather than holding an "other" or team focus. This insight is important, because awareness is a precursor to growth. As you work through the questions, you'll learn more about your deeper self and identify areas where you may want to do some work. Your stand should ultimately suggest those character traits you want to embody, even if you aren't 100 percent there right now.

You'll think of your own questions based on what is important to you as you get rolling—remember this is your stand, not mine.

Try to come up with six to ten statements that feel really powerful and right for you.

Part 2: Define Your Values

The second part of this is to clarify your values so you can become the kind of person who can stand his or her ground every day. Values answer the question "What do I want more of or less of in my life?"

Often leadership experts will have you rank values and try to pare it down to a top five or six. Most people come up with such values as leadership, teamwork, family, and faith. My feeling is that, for the Way of the SEAL, these are a given. In this exercise, I'd like you to focus on more intimate values that will make you a better, stronger person. By identifying and then practicing them, you will habituate yourself to the values and turn them into virtues deeply embedded into your character, as opposed to simply words on a list.

Write down those things you would like to move toward, and a few things you would like to move away from. To guide you, here are my values for living a good life, phrased according to what I want to be more like (you can also just list the base values themselves, for example, health and positivity, love and passion, etc.):

- healthy and positive
- loving and passionate
- wise and authentic
- grateful and truthful
- playful and fun
- learning and growing
- bold and decisive
- contributing to others

Examples of "less of" values from my list include:

- negative and judgmental
- attached and cluttered
- selfish

You can gain tremendous momentum in transformation if you list small actions moving you toward or away from each value. For example, I move toward "healthy and positive" whenever I eat well, hydrate, think of my health, meditate, or train. Such small steps make it easy for me to turn the values of health and positivity into a habit, thus forging new character traits.

Part 3: Discover Your Passion

Now let's do some fun fantasizing. The reason you want to clarify what you're passionate about is so you can put energy toward doing more of it, which will help keep you motivated toward positive change! Your passions are the answer to "Who am I at my deepest level?" Chances are, your passions point the way toward your purpose, the end goal of this exercise. So out of this will emerge a commitment to start, or deepen, your involvement in an activity that is very meaningful and rewarding to you. In addition, it will help you identify your purpose so you can align your activities with it to achieve satisfaction, success, and significance.

Start by asking yourself the questions below. Ask them one at a time and write down whatever comes to you. Remember: Pay attention to your first impressions and try not to judge.

1. What books, movies, art, or music get you pumped?

2. Who inspires you and why?

3. What characteristics of yours make you feel great about yourself?

4. What activities would you do if you had more time and no barriers?

5. What is meaningful to you about these activities?

6. What benefit to others would these activities or characteristics provide?

7. Could you change the world, making it even a tiny bit better, by focusing more on these?

8. What would it take to get you to step into the arena of even just one of these activities?

As with writing your stand, if you find your answers skewing negatively—for example, if you see no benefit to others in your activities or don't see yourself affecting change in the world in even a small way—you've stumbled upon an opportunity for deep reflection. What's really motivating you in life?

Part 4: Uncover Your Purpose

This final step is often the most difficult for my trainees. For maximum effect, I encourage you to investigate a "being" purpose. For instance, my first articulated purpose was to be a warrior leader and to master myself so that I could fulfill that purpose to the best of my ability. Along the way to fulfilling that purpose, I naturally included some goals that focused on external achievements, such as earning the Navy SEAL Trident (representing graduation from the arduous two-year training pipeline), leading a SEAL Platoon, and becoming an expert trainer. However, these weren't my primary focus. My purpose centered on a concept of self-transformation, of becoming something at the character level, not on the mere acquisition of a title or position. I did not choose as my purpose "to become a SEAL officer, attaining the rank of admiral." Even though it technically includes "being" something, this kind of purpose puts your focus only on the label, not the contents within.

Why is the focus of your purpose so important? Because you don't know what twists and turns will occur on your journey. Stating a "being" purpose will provide you with direction and an intrinsic motivation for your journey while allowing flexibility, spontaneity, and change to occur along the way. Stating an "achievement" purpose will only lock you into a narrowly defined role and lead to disappointment when things don't work out the way you imagined.

Armed with your new self-awareness from Parts 1 to 3, contemplate all the possibilities that look, feel, or sound as if they're in line with your passion, values, and stand. In my twenties, I was passionate about personal growth, fitness, adventure, leadership, and the martial arts. When I looked within and sought my purpose, I naturally started to imagine careers similar to the first vision I imagined after happening upon the "Be Someone Special" poster about the SEALs. I saw myself doing jobs that were adventurous, provided risky and messy leadership opportunities, placed a high value on physical preparedness, and connected in some way to what I believed a warrior would do. I came up with several military and commercial options, but in the end, I stayed firm in my focus on the SEALs. Later on, as my internal awareness expanded, I began to connect to an even deeper, intrinsically motivated purpose. Today my purpose is "to attain self-mastery and let truth, wisdom, and love flow through me. To be an inspiration for others through my example and teaching, facilitating personal and global transformation in the process."

Take time now to write a few sentences or paragraphs defining your purpose in life. Come back to it often and refine it as your insights roll in. I check in with my purpose daily. Often I find myself changing a proposed action I had planned or even a word in my statement. All of these—your stand, values, passion, and even your purpose—are subject to grow and change as you do, so don't try to set them in concrete lest you get stuck in there with them!

ENVISION YOUR "FUTURE ME"

When you're satisfied with your results from the previous assessments, it's time to develop an internal representation of you at your absolute finest as a human, designed around fulfilling your purpose, living with passion and in alignment with your values, all while standing your ground. Doing so will reinforce your self-discovery process and give you a stimulating, motivating vision to remind you why you're doing all this work! It'll also start to build your visualization muscles, something we'll develop throughout this book.

One of my most powerful experiences with visualization came in my early twenties. When I still hadn't received an acceptance to OCS nine months after quitting my job in New York, my winning attitude started to falter. To stop the downward slide from discouragement to depression and eventually giving up, I began a rigorous mental regimen of visualization, designed to give me a concrete mental and emotional map to becoming a man worthy of wearing the Trident. I needed a visual baseline, so armed with the SEAL recruiting video *Be Someone Special*, I followed the instructions I shared with you in Part 1 of the WOS Assessment exercise for getting comfortable and breathing deeply, and then I closed my eyes and inserted myself into a mental version of the video. There I was—running, diving, shooting, rappelling, and paddling small boats through the surf zone. Each time I did this, I saw myself succeeding at a high level in each activity. I went so far as to have dialogues with other SEALs and instructors in my mind. The story became more real every time I practiced. I even visualized the moment I received my Trident, down to the time of day, the warmth of the sun shining down, the sound of the crowd, and how it would all feel.

After about six months of daily practice, I felt a shift. Subtle at first, it grew more intense as I poured more energy into my mental practice. (Visualization for skill rehearsal led to serious improvements in my physical performance also, but we'll discuss that with Principle 3.) Any uncertainty about my chances of becoming a SEAL disappeared. It no longer felt like hope, but more like my destiny! This fueled my efforts to get even better prepared physically than other candidates and to convince the recruiter I was SEAL material. Soon my stats put me at the top of the heap and I earned my recruiter's endorsement. At age twenty-five and with no prior military experience, I was one of a small handful admitted to OCS with a SEAL contract that year.

Even though you may not feel or look the part now, you must envision yourself in your ideal state, activating your personal power and living in alignment with your stand and purpose. I learned in the SEALs that there's no such thing as perfection, only perfect effort. Through practicing a "perfect" version of ourselves mentally, we'll slowly become that person in real life.

Step 1: Find a comfortable place to sit with your journal—I encourage you to use the same space you used for your WOS Assessment, a place that can become your "sit space" or meditation room. Close your eyes and breathe with deep abdominal breaths for at least five minutes. While breathing, just relax. After at least five minutes of deep breathing, begin the visualization as described below.

Step 2: In your mind's eye, conjure up an image of you in your ideal state three months from now. See yourself as having already accomplished your intermediate goals, in perfect health, and fully embodying the character traits that represent your stand, values, and purpose. As this image becomes clear, add color, sound, emotions, and movement to it, as if you were watching yourself in a movie. This process should take only a couple minutes.

Step 3: Now fast forward and repeat the imagery, but from the point of view of one year out. Then, if you desire, take it out three years and repeat.

Step 4: When you are satisfied with your "Future Me" visions, collapse them all to the present moment and see yourself now as that person. See yourself as someone who has already earned your personal Trident. Own it and breathe into that vision. When you are done, simply open your eyes and carry on with your day, leaving your subconscious mind to do its part.

DEVELOP FRONT-SIGHT FOCUS

Keep your eyes trained on the front sight and your
front sight trained on the target.
—SEAL INSTRUCTOR

In the pitch black, the sound of the helicopter's rotor blades was deafening. The jumpmaster gave us the thumbs-up as the light turned green. I leaped out into the dark. The static line did its job and pulled my main chute from its rig. I counted one thousand one, one thousand two, one thousand three, and looked up to check the canopy. *Whew. Everything looks A-OK.*

Ahead in the darkness I could see the vague outline of my teammate Chris's canopy. Something was wrong. I took a closer look—yep, he was coming toward me. Standard operating procedure for potential midair collisions is for both jumpers to pull their right toggles, thereby moving them away from each other. I turned right. Chris turned left and collided with me.

My canopy collapsed into a wobbly sheet. I began plummeting to the earth, picking up speed. I had about eight seconds remaining in my 26-year-old life.

My mind slowed. My breathing slowed. Time even slowed. Each second seemed like a minute as I moved through the malfunction checklist: Pull on riser to try to reinflate canopy (nothing). Pull on reserve chute cord, punch the bag and rip the reserve out, and throw it as hard possible into the wind (no good—the reserve shot up and waffled a bit around the main). *I'm screwed.* I took another deep breath and shook the risers of the canopy again. I said my goodbyes and prayed I'd lived a good enough life that the next few moments would come with white light instead of fire.

Suddenly the chute caught some air, and then I hit the ground like a ton of bricks. The canopy had only partially inflated, but it was enough to slow me down for a survivable landing. I waited a moment and took a deep breath to confirm I was still alive. I scanned my body for broken bones. Amazingly unscathed, I got up, dusted myself off, and marched off to find Chris so I could deck him.

What stuck with me most from this experience was how my training kicked in, allowing me to perform under extremely stressful conditions. Things felt almost mystical as my mind slowed down and allowed a larger intelligence and calmness to flow through me. I know I would've died if I'd tried to think my way out. My front-sight focus, combined with unconscious competence developed by relentless and realistic training, had saved my life.

In my own training programs, I use the term "front-sight focus" to describe the incredible concentration and single-mindedness SEALs tap into when pursuing a target, whether they're aiming a weapon at a terrorist, planning a raid, or methodically working through a mess when things go wrong! Front-sight focus refers to a shooter gazing intently at the front sight on his weapon after lining it up with his target. When you do this, you remain super aware of your surroundings and have your objective in your mind, but your attention narrows down to that piece of metal just a few inches in front of you. Compare that precise effort to working with a more "shotgun" approach of aiming in the direction of your target and firing, hoping some of your scattered shots will strike.

Maintaining a front-sight focus has a calming and confidence-building effect. A SEAL knows he must simply engage one target at a time and not shift focus until he's dispatched that target. SEALs don't like to waste ammo—we try to make each round count. This is far more effective than trying to engage multiple targets (or worry about them all at the same time!). Admittedly, our training allows us to do this very fast and with incredible precision, making it appear as if we're tackling multiple targets simultaneously. Ultimately, all great successes follow this exact process: Identify a goal, and then achieve it by knocking down one target after another, each one the right target for that shot. When you learn to do this with the focus and precision of a SEAL, understanding which targets to engage and how to avoid distractions, your success will skyrocket.

In SEAL-speak, your goals typically come in two types: You have your big, long-term goals defining your end state, and you have shorter-term subgoals defining your path along the way. The former we refer to as the overall mission, while the latter are your targets (your efforts to achieve each target are also interim missions, though typically smaller in scope or shorter in length). SEALs work on one mission at a time, though there may be multiple targets to achieve overall mission success. Whether you face immediate challenges or need a lasting long-term strategy, you can overcome any obstacle and achieve any goal with front-sight focus through a four-pronged approach:

- prepare your mind
- envision your goal
- define the mission
- simplify the battlefield

Though most people will never face the risk of plummeting to earth in a compromised parachute jump, we all have major challenges to overcome. When you practice front-sight focus in your life, you'll easily distinguish high-value targets from low-hanging fruit and maintain total confidence as you move toward these targets amid any amount of turbulence. You'll also develop a habit of simplicity, which will reduce said turbulence and enhance the results of any pursuit. Without front-sight focus, you're bound to get derailed and end up mired in common, day-to-day activities and thinking. Common thinking in combat can get you killed, but in everyday life, it will simply kill any chance of your operating at the high level we expect for the Way of the SEAL.

Prepare Your Mind

Victorious warriors win first in their minds, and then go to war.
Defeated warriors go to war first and then seek to win.
—Sun Tzu, author of *The Art of War* (544 BCE–496 BCE)

I was on the training floor at Seido Karate, where Grandmaster Nakamura had invited me to test for my black belt. Things started innocuously—my two classmates and I had to demonstrate all the katas and self-defense moves from white belt through advanced brown. No problem. Then Nakamura threw a curveball: He asked us to get our sparring gear on while a long line of scary-looking senior black belts filed into the room. I panicked, thinking, "Uh-oh, this can't be good." Apparently, word had gone out that we needed to learn some lessons, and there were plenty of masters willing to help.

I dug into my first match trying to recall all the moves I'd learned over the past four years and a thousand hours of training, but I was up against fighters with far more skill. I got my butt handed to me. I was tough, though, and two hours later, I was still fighting. My body pushed to exhaustion, I recall vividly the moment things shifted. Sensei Leyton, renowned for his relentlessness as a fighter, was taking his second turn dishing it out to me. He exploited my weaknesses, laying me on my back twice. Energy waning, I began to wonder: Perhaps this test had less to do with my physical skill and more to do with the mental, emotional, and spiritual skills refined during our "inner" training at Seido. I knew I had to tap into my training at an entirely different level and stop fighting a physical fight.

I started breathing deeply and shouted an internal command to my exhausted body: "NOW!" I opened my eyes wide and stopped worrying about the weaponlike fists and feet coming at me, instead focusing on my opponent's vital areas one at a time as these targets entered my awareness. The deep breathing slowed my heart rate and relaxed my muscles; my mind entered a meditative state. Time slowed, my internal chatter calmed, and I was able to face my fear with an unfettered mind. Something clicked deep inside as a calm courage backed by a rush of energy surged through me. I began fighting with a newfound force and control. Soon my rejuvenated fighting spirit, flowing from deep within, got the attention of Grandmaster Nakamura, who shouted, "ENOUGH!"

Nakamura (with the help of what seemed like every senior black belt in New York City) took me to the edge physically, but I had to let go of the distracting chatter of my "thinking" mind, which was slowing me down, to radically focus my whole being on victory. I finally stopped thinking about the test, worrying about how well I was doing and what moves I should make next. I became front-sight focused on hitting just one target at a time—landing a strike or blocking a move—and found I could more easily tap into the mental toughness and spiritual strength I needed to succeed. As I earned my black belt, I stumbled upon what would eventually become the first tenet of maintaining front-sight focus: To win at anything, we must first win control over our minds.

Deep Breathing

Before you can take control of your mind, you must first calm it down. The fastest way to calm your mind, along with your body, is through slow and controlled deep breathing. Deep diaphragmatic breathing, set to a rhythm appropriate for your situation, is a simple but powerful tool for controlling your physiological response. By focusing on your breath, you collapse your focus to the "front sight" that is the present moment. This settling practice helps reduce mental chatter, prevents your mind from wandering, and is generally a great boost to your self-control efforts. It will also rebalance your nervous system and reduce harmful physiological effects associated with fear and stress.

In Principle 5, we'll discuss how to train this skill as one of five crucial elements for mental toughness, but for now let's take a moment to experience its effects with a quick drill.

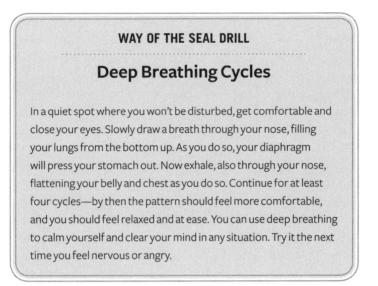

WAY OF THE SEAL DRILL

Deep Breathing Cycles

In a quiet spot where you won't be disturbed, get comfortable and close your eyes. Slowly draw a breath through your nose, filling your lungs from the bottom up. As you do so, your diaphragm will press your stomach out. Now exhale, also through your nose, flattening your belly and chest as you do so. Continue for at least four cycles—by then the pattern should feel more comfortable, and you should feel relaxed and at ease. You can use deep breathing to calm yourself and clear your mind in any situation. Try it the next time you feel nervous or angry.

The Sacred Silence

Another thing I learned while training at Seido Karate, reinforced many times in the SEALs, was the power of silence to set the conditions to win in my mind. Silence can come in the form of seated meditation, like Zen training, or sitting in a hide site observing a target for twenty-four hours. I saw a huge drop in my opportunities to experience silence after returning to the business world from active duty. In fact, when I first left active duty and started pursuing some business ventures, I got away from practicing my martial arts and silence altogether. I had a difficult time controlling my mind and emotions. As a result, I found myself easily distracted, often lost my front-sight focus, and failed to listen to my gut and make "hard-right" choices.

My eagerness to get into business led me to launch NavySEALs.com in the same period that I agreed to partner with my brothers-in-law to start a brewpub. Up to my eyeballs in the brewpub venture, I couldn't give NavySEALs.com the time and energy it deserved, so in a hasty decision I gave 50 percent interest to a web developer who would build the site and run the business for us. Without a sacred silence practice, I too easily suppressed my concerns that, though he was a great, well-intentioned guy, my new partner's passion for design outweighed his business acumen. Sure enough, the resulting site looked cool but didn't earn a dime.

I bought him out, but, once again ignoring my gut and feeling overwhelmed, I rushed into outsourcing the site's management to another web development company without performing a thorough background check. Things started well, but communication broke down when I discovered their efforts to hijack my domain name. I again took immediate action to end the relationship, and they responded by stealing the entire framework and intellectual property of NavySEALs.com to launch an exact replica of my business. Boy, did I feel foolish, especially since the brewpub had started devolving into a quagmire during these same few months. If I had taken the time to meditate during that period, I would have recognized how my anxiety distracted me and negatively influenced my decisions. I would then have focused on relieving my anxiety so I could better concentrate on the right targets and hit them in quick succession. Instead, I found myself reacting to failure, trying to make one-off "saves" while getting further and further off-course.

Once I understood what had led me astray during these months, I vowed never to turn my back on my training again. I believe strongly that WOS leaders must structure sacred silence time for themselves and their team daily.

Silence creates the space for you to think and thus see reality more clearly, which is crucial for you to train your front-sight focus on your targets and stay on mission. With practice, we can gain complete control over the critical mind (the one that incorrectly inflates or deflates us) and tap into our fuller mental powers. In addition to better seeing our true selves, we also better see reality with a clear, still mind, so we make improved decisions and gain more insight. When I first started meditating under Nakamura's guidance, I could barely maintain a silent mind for two breath cycles. I thought about my unhappy work life, my MBA projects, my girlfriend, and just about everything else. It was only after six months of training that I was able to quiet my mind for four or five breath cycles, an achievement that rewarded me with new insights, some of which—such as the realization that my job was making me miserable and had no meaningful purpose to me besides money and credentials—led me to question my choices. After more than a year in weekly silent practice, I could reach ten breath cycles, and I saw clearly that my dissatisfaction came not from my unhappy job, but from not aligning with my unique purpose in life.

Another example comes from one of my students. Severely depressed after the death of his brother, twenty-something Zach was in desperate straits when he stumbled upon SEALFIT and joined my Unbeatable Mind program. Zach and his brother Chris were very close, spending many hours together hiking and on long motorcycle rides. During one such ride together, Chris died in an accident. Naturally, Zach felt the loss acutely, blaming himself for not being able to protect his brother. Survivor guilt is not uncommon, but it hit Zach especially hard as he did not have the support or tools to deal with it very well. Therapy didn't help much and prescription drugs just allowed him to slide deeper into a smothering depression. A former top athlete, he lost his front-sight focus on his physical goals and became very lethargic, having trouble just getting out of bed some days. It got so bad he considered taking his own life.

One day a concerned friend introduced him to SEALFIT and my free online video training. Desperate for answers, Zach started by simply listening to the motivational video messages. He began to feel his mental state shifting just from feeding it these few positive messages and from the no-nonsense approach they emphasized. He tried one of the free physical training videos and felt so good afterward that it immediately hooked him. He soon became a client of my Unbeatable Mind online program, which led him to the next level of his healing.

Front-sight focus requires leaning into your mission with confidence and clarity, so the very first lesson of the Unbeatable Mind course is all about developing mental control. It includes a silence practice I call

Still Water Runs Deep, a combination of meditation and visualization named after one of Grandmaster Nakamura's Zen lectures, which I attended every Thursday evening prior to our meditation sessions back at Seido Karate. The still water metaphor represents the deep, ever-present witnessing of the self or soul, normally drowned out by the turbulent rapids of one's critical mind. Zach latched on to this practice, his first exposure to sacred silence. At first, he struggled as much as I did back in the dojo in New York—it's difficult work, especially for active folks, to sit in silence and still the thinking mind.

WAY OF THE SEAL DRILL

Still Water Runs Deep

Sitting in a chair or against the wall, ensure that your back is straight, your chin is slightly tucked, and you're comfortable. Now gently close your eyes and bring your awareness to your breathing. Go through five cycles of deep breathing as described earlier, visualizing your body calming down from head to toes. After this, release into a natural breathing pattern but maintain focus on your breath.

In your mind's eye, see yourself sitting at the bottom of a deep pond. Feel the serenity and silence as you look around and up at the clear, sparkling water of the surface. Any thoughts that arise are mere ripples. After a while, if you choose, you can let this vision dissolve and just focus on your breathing. Now, start counting each breath cycle. If, after two counts, you suddenly realize you've been thinking about a big project at work, no worries. Just let it float to the surface and dissolve, then start the count over. Your objective is to get to ten without any conscious thought. This is much more difficult than it sounds! Practice for five minutes at least once a day for thirty days. Once you feel you are well on your way to quieting your mind, you can blend this with other practices in this book.

It took him a few months of practicing fifteen minutes daily before he was slowly able to settle his mind and bring it under control. As he became more reflective and insightful, he was able to detach from the negative mental chatter and painful emotions that had kept him locked in an obsessive loop of guilt and loss. He saw how he hadn't allowed himself to go through the normal grieving process because he partly blamed himself for his brother's death. It was during his Still Water sessions that he first became aware of his innate goodness as a person and as a brother, which rekindled his ability to love and forgive himself. The deeper connection to his spirit cultivated during these training sessions also gave rise to crucial insights, such as understanding and accepting that there was nothing he could have done to save Chris, and that the best way to honor his brother would be to live a healthy, happy life, not a broken one. Through this simple but effective practice, Zach began to heal himself from within.

After several more months of training, he added a positivity practice and rewired his subconscious with the powerful mantra, "Day by day, in every way, I am getting better and better" (a classic I recommend in the Unbeatable Mind program) and also "I am a good person and my brother loves me." He supported these mantras with positive imagery, envisioning himself as a supportive and loving brother, and seeing his brother in a good place now, full of forgiveness. Soon he found the energy and motivation to step up his physical training using SEALFIT yoga and functional fitness training.

Two years later, Zach approached me after the closing ceremony of one of my 20X Challenge events. He told me that Unbeatable Mind training, in particular the Still Water practice, had saved his life! Regaining control of his mind helped him divert energy previously going toward "black holes" of negative thought and behavior and redirect it toward a front-sight focus on positive goals, like improving his health. Now he's superfit and well adjusted, and the huge smile on his face said it all. He had resolved his guilt around his brother's death and said he now felt better than he had in years. As he told me his story,

I felt a wave of gratitude wash over me. Zach just needed someone to show him how to settle his mind and connect with his inner nature, where goodness and love reside. Fear and negativity cannot exist in the presence of love. Every one of us has this inner nature, and it's time to slow down and connect with it!

In the Exercises section of this chapter I'll give you some advanced tools for getting control of your mind and retraining your thoughts, but it's important you begin a sacred silence practice right away. Whatever you are struggling with in your life, you can use this quick and simple drill to set the stage to win in your mind.

Envision Your Goal

What the mind of man can conceive and believe, he can achieve.
—NAPOLEON HILL, BESTSELLING AUTHOR OF
THINK AND GROW RICH (1883–1970)

Front-sight focus, especially when backed up by a powerful and clear set point, can propel you toward each target on your way to mission success. But what exactly are you supposed to focus on? How do you "see" your target of, say, completing a certification crucial for your next promotion, or your mission of finding a loving partner and building a family? The key is to envision your goal—whether at the target or mission level—using a type of visualization called "mental projection." With Principle 1, I shared my "Future Me" visualization practice, which is one kind of mental projection. The purpose of this type of visualization is to plant seeds of a future desired state, such as becoming CEO of your company, into your subconscious mind and nervous system. As you take action in the "real world," the new inner vision will align your heart and mind with your actions and support your efforts to achieve that desired state. In other words, mental projections combined with real action form a process of seeing, believing, and making it happen, an incredibly simple but profound concept that has led to significant breakthroughs in my life and with my students as well.

See It, Believe It, Make It Happen

Jim came to SEALFIT Academy in 2011 and proved to me once again the power of mental projections. At the time, Jim had just turned forty and worked as a regional sales rep for a manufacturing company. He was not satisfied with his life, though he had a good job, financial security, and a great family. I hear this story so often, I feel like it's a national "dis-ease." Jim had learned about SEALFIT from a friend, and he felt the training would help jolt him out of his flatline lifestyle and propel him into a more purposeful existence.

At the Academy, my staff and I forced him to sit in silence, to clarify and write down his stand, and to state his purpose and passion. Within days, he came to the realization that he was, as I was in my twenties, misaligned. Jim was entrenched in an industrial sales job that had nothing to do with his passion of teaching and leading others. He wanted to teach others the SEALFIT model for its hands-on, warrior-athlete approach. However, Jim was just learning the nuts and bolts. He understood that, as Gandhi said, he must "be the change he would like to see in the world," so he decided on the spot to work hard to change himself first. But, he asked me, beyond learning the external skills of SEALFIT, how and where should he start training?

I advised Jim to first clarify his purpose, to write it down, and then get front-sight focused on his mission to align his life with his new purpose. He came back to me the next day and said that his purpose was to inspire others to higher levels of achievement and to love life and live it honorably. He'd identified a mission as well: To open a training facility in his hometown to teach SEALFIT methods and values, especially honor. The cool thing was that this wasn't about changing his career or leaving a dead-end job. In fact, Jim planned to stay in his job so he could support his family even while he pursued his new dream. No, it was about having an impact on the world in a way that was meaningful to him outside of his job. His new mission had to run parallel with his means of earning an income. This is a great example of how a mature, family-oriented man or woman could apply the principles of change and alignment when his or her risk factor is so much higher than, say, that of a twenty-four-year-old CPA looking over the fence at the SEALs.

I knew Jim needed to see his outcome clearly in his mind to set the conditions for his personal victory. I had him create vivid images of what this success would look like in two years. He took my recommendations to heart and began an earnest daily practice of visualization using his mind gym (which you'll learn to build in the Exercises section of this chapter). He envisioned his ideal training facility, the type of members he had, what classes he would host, how he would finance and run the operation, and the impact it would have on his family, especially his kids. He decided he wouldn't run the gym himself, instead letting his wife manage the place, as she was very interested in being involved. In his visualizations, the two of them worked side by side and even had the kids involved as much as possible, the whole family as a team made stronger in the process. With the seed planted, he left SEALFIT to go back to his daily grind, but he continued the daily visualization practice (along with many of the other things he learned, such as the use of focus plans, which I provide for you in Appendix 1) and didn't let the vision slide back into the primordial soup from which it arose.

As he continued the internal work, it soon began to bear its magical fruit. Jim gained tremendous confidence that the gym he envisioned was not a fantasy, but already a reality. He just needed to take action to bring it to fruition. With a full-time job, travel requirements, and a family to feed, Jim still never lost his focus on the goal and methodically executed the plan he had first envisioned at SEALFIT, including getting more certifications, saving the money, securing the location, and doing all he needed to ensure his vision would come true. Sure enough, two years after I met him, he invited me to present an Unbeatable Mind seminar at CrossFit Honor, his new gym in his hometown of Allentown, Pennsylvania.

When I met the members of CrossFit Honor, the full weight of Jim's accomplishments humbled me. These folks were incredibly passionate about the culture, the community they were creating, and the training. Jim had created exactly what he had envisioned and transformed the energy of his vision into a membership of 130 warriors living the SEALFIT values. His lovely wife was running the gym, and his twelve-year-old son eagerly participated in the workouts, doing pull-ups, push-ups, and air squats along with the adult athletes in the class. No question that Jim saw it and believed it, aligned his passion and purpose, visualized it daily, then made it happen in the most important of ways—through helping others.

WAY OF THE SEAL DRILL

Fantasizing with Purpose

- **Step 1: "See" it.** You'll need to get clear about your desired outcome. We'll discuss how to plan your mission in the next chapter, but for now just focus on defining where you want to end up.

- **Step 2: Imagine it.** Like Jim, you must imagine the outcome as if you've already achieved it. Most people can fantasize; with envisioning, you're creating a purposeful fantasy. This step requires a baseline reference to ground it in reality: Establish a visual reference point (to make your fantasy more concrete) and insert yourself into the imagery. References can be actual experiences, still photographs, or moving images (like my use of the SEALs' *Be Someone Special* video).

- **Step 3: Practice it.** Play your imagined reality in your mind daily. I recommend you do it as part of a powerful Morning or Evening Ritual (found in Appendix 2). For maximum effectiveness, you must infuse your visualization with belief, expectation, and an intense desire to bring the visualized event to life.

The tenets introduced so far in this chapter are just the starting point. Preparing the right conditions in your mind will empower your efforts toward any important goal in your life. You have to know where you're headed if you're going to move forward with SEAL-worthy front-sight focus. But how do you avoid pitfalls and other distractions on your way from point A to point B? You must ensure that you've clearly defined the mission and then simplify the battlefield so nothing stands in your way.

Define the Mission

A chain is only as strong as its weakest link.
—PROVERB

When you strive to achieve any goal (read: embark on a mission), you must clarify and define expectations, both explicit and implicit. You may have a good handle on the explicit expectations, such as "get the business up and running on time and within budget." However, hidden within any mission are also implicit expectations.

For example, a SEAL may explicitly define his mission as the sinking of an enemy ship. Implied in the mission, however, may be that the upper echelon leaders expect the SEALs to put the ship out of commission for at least six months, complete the mission in secret that evening, and do it without any losses. If the implied tasks of the mission are out of sync with the Team's competencies, resources, risk tolerance, or time frame, then it will fail.

Let's say the explicit task is to launch a new product line. Seems straightforward, right? However, what's implied is that we understand the market's needs, what drives our customers' purchasing patterns, how to develop the product, and how to market the line effectively to our niche. Sometimes implicit tasks may lie outside the scope of your core skills or comfort zone, so you'd have to completely reeducate yourself or retool your business to accomplish the overall mission. Asking good questions keeps you from overcommitting to missions you can't or shouldn't complete, which by their very nature undermine your front-sight focus. Proper planning from the start will help prevent sudden and unfavorable consequences later, which could interfere with your ability to maintain front-sight focus on missions you've accepted or chosen.

Soon after developing my Unbeatable Mind training, for example, I decided I wanted to deliver a digital format via the web. I defined the mission as creating video and audio of the program and, within a self-imposed sixty-day timeline, start selling the first lesson of the program through a new subscription website. I felt certain this mission aligned with our overall company vision, and, as my top priority, it commanded my complete focus. The explicit tasks were achievable, but there were a few implicit tasks I uncovered in the questioning process that prompted me to change the mission. First, the plan required expert sales copy designed for an Internet campaign, a skill my marketing department lacked. To pull the mission off, I would need to source a professional copywriter, which I soon learned was neither cheap nor easy to find. In addition, I had to define and establish the sales process, the marketing message, and an e-mail-marketing engine. To accomplish these things, I realized that my team and I would need education on partner and affiliate marketing, brand-new business skills that could take months to master. Additionally, there were legal issues around the process of selling digital content in subscription format that would further delay the launch while we found an attorney who understood the language. All of these implicit tasks required that I step back from my initial scope and timeline, redefine the overall mission, and then temporarily shift my front-sight focus to work through the preparatory stages I'd identified as necessary to reach my end-goal.

WAY OF THE SEAL DRILL

Question the Mission

To get clear on the implicit tasks your leaders are asking you to do (or what you're asking of yourself), you must ask deeper questions, such as:

- Why am I doing this? Is it aligned with our overall mission as a company/team?

- Is there some higher priority project that may take precedence and sidetrack me?

- Who else, if anyone, is involved in getting this project done?

- What exactly is expected of me and any others who may be involved?

- How and when can I count on them to fulfill their commitments?

- What other subtasks are required before I can fulfill what's expected of me?

- What other tasks are required in order for me to accomplish this mission?

Simplify the Battlefield

Simple can be harder than complex: You have to work hard to get your thinking clean to make it simple. But it's worth it in the end because once you get there, you can move mountains.

—STEVE JOBS, AMERICAN ENTREPRENEUR
AND CO-FOUNDER OF APPLE, INC. (1955-2011)

"Simplifying the battlefield" is SEAL-speak for eliminating distractions. When we eliminate distractions, we can better see the simple, elegant solutions and remain front-sight focused on the right way forward. Even elite teams can get distracted and veer toward the complex. Steve Jobs is famous for telling his design teams, "Not simple enough." He insisted on single-button operation for the groundbreaking iPhone, for example, with the full features accessed via software icons. Prior to the iPhone, smartphones like the BlackBerry required a multitude of buttons to access myriad features. Jobs relentlessly pushed for simplicity, and the results speak for themselves. Legend has it he later handed an iPad (which has the same features as the iPhone) to a preschool kid in Africa who had never even held a phone, let alone a high-tech tablet. The kid was able to turn it on and, swiping away, access its full features without any instruction.

Simplifying the battlefield requires two key elements. First, you must know your unique offer as an individual, team, or business so you can identify what you must do and what you can delegate to others. Then you must declutter your internal and external environments so you can see simple solutions more easily.

Determine Your Unique Offer

Understanding your unique offer as an individual is easy if you've defined your purpose and your stand. If you're currently in a leadership position, you must also understand your team's or business's unique offer to the world—your special capability.

The SEAL skill set includes many talents, such as special reconnaissance, foreign internal defense, counterterrorism, security details, military-diplomatic liaison, and more. However, the Teams understand and try hard to remain focused on their unique offer, which is their ability to neutralize the enemy through direct action (read: get in, get it done, and get out). How do you determine your unique offer? Similar to defining your purpose, the process begins with penetrating questions, such as:

- What am I exceptionally good at and passionate about doing?
- What one thing (individually, or as a team or organization) do I or we do better than everyone else does?

- What qualities do I possess that give rise to or support this unique offer?
- Who benefits most from this capability?
- How would I benefit if I could deliver more of this unique value? Would I or we be better off?
- What actions can I take right now to eliminate the things distracting me from delivering my unique offer?

These are just guides, so don't hesitate to use questions more germane to your situation. The point is to get to the core of what we do and who we are. For example, one of my unique offers is teaching. Some of the qualities I possess that support my teaching ability are my passion for coaching and communicating and a talent for envisioning the future. My students benefit most directly from my instruction, but the more I connect with people who reflect my strengths and weaknesses back to me, the more I learn, as well. On the other hand, I'm not so great at executing day-to-day operations through such activities as web development and Internet marketing. To keep these from distracting me, I must have good managers and technical support teams with those unique offers to do these tasks instead.

Once you're clear on your unique offer, it's time to declutter by eliminating (or, when appropriate, delegating) everything that may distract you. By keeping things simple, your resources can go into a concentrated effort—and this is crucial for dramatic results.

Declutter Your Environment

When your clutter isn't bogging you down, you literally and metaphorically have more room for the things you need. If you eliminate, outsource, and delegate obligations, beliefs, even relationships that no longer suit you, you'll have more resources for your key priorities. When Steve Jobs returned to Apple in 1996 after eleven years of forced absence, he immediately evaluated and identified Apple's unique offer as providing powerful, simple, and elegant computing solutions to a public weary of complicated, boring personal computers. Under his leadership, Apple shed a significant number of products, projects, and entire divisions to focus on the new iMac, which led a new and very narrow range of promising products. The results turned the company around in six months. Similarly, when I committed to writing this book, I shunted 90 percent of my daily business tasks to my team so I could focus on my unique offer of teaching my philosophy and practices. As a result, I was able to focus on the book, and they were empowered to focus on what they do best—running the day-to-day operations of SEALFIT.

Decluttering your environment will also make you lighter internally, allowing you to exercise more control over where, when, and how you make an impact (as well as controlling the character of that impact!). For example, when the Reserves deployed me to Iraq in 2004, to maintain my front-sight focus, I gave up a long-held dream of earning my Ph.D. I had always thought earning my Ph.D. would allow me to reach more people with my leadership philosophy by qualifying me for a professorship. But now, my focus was required elsewhere. Plus, I knew that when I returned home I'd want to focus on my recently launched business, U.S. Tactical, and I had become increasingly aware that my particular brand of leadership development didn't translate well to the academic world. Though it was hard to give up the idea of the Ph.D., I recognized it as a target that no longer fit my life's mission.

I teach a three-part system for keeping things simple: First is to declutter your physical surroundings, and then your commitments, and finally your internal state. I call this the KISS (Keep It Simple, Smarty) exercise and will show you how to do it at the end of this chapter, but here's an overview of how it works.

Kick-start the process by clearing out external spaces such as your closet, garage, car trunk, and desk. Culling the clutter and cleaning out these spaces—which you probably look at or enter daily—can have a tremendous effect on your psyche, helping you release stopped-up energy that's clogging your creative flow. It's like a mental breath of fresh air.

Next, declutter your tasks and commitments by implementing the 80/20 rule. This theory essentially says 20 percent of your actions will lead to 80 percent of your results. If you identify that highly effective 20 percent and eliminate, delegate, or outsource everything else, you can devote more resources to your unique offer and most productive actions.

Once you've simplified your external environment, it becomes easier to simplify your internal environment, perhaps the stickiest part of maintaining front-sight focus. This part is saying goodbye to emotional entanglements or rigid beliefs that weigh you down or hold you back. Take a deep look at any emotional baggage you may have, such as a relationship that isn't working. Then look for beliefs that now clash with your reality, such as if you loved and were exceptional in music but believed you couldn't earn a living in the music field because your father said it wasn't a real job. Many people reach this point and fail to take action because they aren't willing to make hard choices or rock the boat. But what if you're on the wrong boat? If you are, you *should* rock it and fall over, punch a shark in the nose, and then swim to the next boat.

Several times a year I hear from young professionals going through the same mental and emotional struggles I encountered twenty-five years ago. Despite their desperation, many fail to follow their inner voice, even after speaking with me. The force of their habits and the resistance to real change is just too great for them to break free. Joel was different. An investment banker when I met him, he attended Kokoro Camp and caught the SEAL bug. He began following my training and advice religiously and decided to seek an officer slot to the SEAL Teams. Recognizing his uncommon level of commitment, I invited him to intern at the SEALFIT training center in Encinitas, California. He packed up and moved from Chicago to San Diego with his wife, leaving a prestigious high-paying job, his home, and his extended family, and ditched nearly all his possessions to focus his energy on his new goal. Nine months later, the Navy selected Joel to attend Officer Candidate School with a slot at BUDS. By simplifying his life, decluttering everything but the essential, he succeeded where so many others fail.

Another good example of how this concept works is my friend Michelle. About five years ago, she started a nutritional supplement business but soon found the complexity of the business difficult to master with her level experience, level of funding, and somewhat divided attention as she simultaneously pursued the education and training to become a firefighter, a long-held dream of hers. When she connected more deeply to her purpose, she realized her on-the-side efforts needed to become her primary goal. So she simplified by selling the supplement business to her manufacturer, retaining a small stake and part-time role, and turned her focus to serving her community full-time as a first responder.

Many people have great intentions about streamlining commitments or starting new efforts but get derailed because their beliefs hold them back. They're afraid to say no to obligations or they allow others to talk them out of things. Have compassion for others, of course, but remember, front-sight focus requires leaning into your mission with confidence and clarity. Though achieving your goals may not require the kind of extreme simplification and reorganization Joel embraced, the principle remains the same. There's no easy way out, no trick I can offer you. You must accept that your choices may have emotional fallout—people could get upset with you, or you might suffer guilt and pain as you make hard choices. This is the natural result of re-organizing your life, but it's temporary. Embrace the suck and do it.

★ ★ ★ EXERCISES ★ ★ ★

WIN IN YOUR MIND

This exercise will help you build a mental defense against distractions; you must have a clear mind in order to effectively choose and pursue your targets and achieve mission success. Let's set the conditions for you to win in your mind so you can maintain front-sight focus and win in life.

Part 1: The Sentinel at the Gate

In this exercise, you'll set up a mental sentinel to witness what's going on inside your brain. This sentinel will observe and report on any negative or unnecessary thoughts (and there will be a lot of both!).

Find your quiet spot (ideally you'll choose one place where you can do all of your mental work). Sit in a chair, lie down, or sit in any position that allows you to keep your back straight comfortably without fidgeting. Begin this exercise with five minutes of deep breathing, your eyes closed. Mentally watch your breath.

Now, release your focus on the breath and just pay attention to what comes up your mind. This is tricky, but you'll get the hang of it soon. The part of you that is noticing or witnessing your thoughts is your sentinel. If it helps, you can imagine a guard or soldier sitting at the control panel of your consciousness, scanning your input and output. When your sentinel notices that you're thinking of something, don't fight it—acknowledge it, let it go, and return to witnessing your thoughts. Are they positive or negative? Are they random or directed? This is important for what follows. You can repeat this part of the exercise several times before moving on to Part 2.

Part 2: DIRECT Your Mind

This is your express train to mental control. Now that you're developing the capacity to observe the inner workings of your mind, we want your sentinel to start directing your thought traffic. Return to your quiet spot. This time, as random thoughts bubble up, implement the DIRECT process below. When you feel comfortable with this powerful method, try to DIRECT your thoughts during the day, especially those destructive to your wellbeing and front-sight focus.

Detect. Your sentinel will detect any thoughts that slip into your mind. Though we'd like to believe our thoughts are under our control, guess again. Thoughts arise constantly, and many have no business being in our minds, nor do they have a positive purpose in our lives. Road rage, what goes through your mind when someone cuts you off in traffic, is a good example of an emotion-driven thought. This happens to the best of us, but every thought distracting your front-sight focus depletes your energy and must be dealt with.

Interdict. If your sentinel detects a negative or useless thought, interdict it with a simple command such as "Stop!" or "No!" When you tell yourself to stop thinking something, guess what? You'll stop . . . for a moment.

Redirect. Once you stop a negative thought, you have to redirect your mind to new, empowering thoughts. When another driver cuts you off, triggering thoughts of revenge, your sentinel detects and then interdicts with "Stop!" The redirect occurs with a short dialogue, such as "Too bad that guy's having a bad day, but I'm not going to let him ruin mine. I'm focusing on the positive now." Your mind will welcome the new, positive direction.

Energize. Solidify the new thought by getting your whole being to support it, entering a new physiological state that matches your mental shift. For example, conjure images of yourself looking strong, confident, and positive. Now, feel it! Sit up straight, break a big smile, and laugh. Breathe deeply and feel the strong, confident, and positive energy course through your body. No one can spoil your good mood!

Communicate. This step is an insurance policy: You must talk to yourself in a new way to override any lurking negativity and prevent new destructive thoughts from creeping in. In SEAL training, I used the mantra, "Feeling good, looking good, ought to be in Hollywood!" to maintain my energy and focus in the grind. I have also used, "Day by day, in every way, I am getting better and better."

Train. Your mind can be a powerful ally or a slothful fiend. Practice the DIRECT technique daily like you would exercise your body (I'll show you how in "Training in the Way of the SEAL"), and it will not only give you control in the moment but also train your mind to function at an elite level permanently.

BUILD YOUR MIND GYM

To develop your visualization skills and to give structure, focus, and momentum to your practice, we're going to build a gym in your mind, a special room where you will do your mental training. Eventually, visiting your mind gym will become a habit that will immediately center you and help you maintain front-sight focus, channeling all your willpower and energy toward whatever you seek to achieve. It's particularly useful as framework for your mental projections.

Find a comfortable position, close your eyes, and let the world begin to fade away. Take a few deep breaths to center yourself. Focus on the breath as it enters and leaves your body. In and out . . . in and out. Follow your breath to stillness. Bring your awareness to the here and now, and let all thoughts and worries of the day, all noisy distractions around you, just flow on through your mind without taking hold. Let it all go.

Now image yourself walking down a path. You are not in a hurry, but you see a set of stairs off to the right in the distance. You walk to the stairs and turn to look down. There are ten steps. You slowly walk down, taking a full breath with each step. Ten, nine, eight . . . When you reach the bottom you see an archway. This is the door to your training area, where you will build your mind gym. You take another breath and step through the door.

You are now in your special training area. It may look familiar to you. Look around and behold the beautiful surroundings. Whatever shows up for you is okay—it may be a beach, a mountain, or a valley. It may not even seem to be from this planet. In this place of yours, gravity has no effect, and you can do anything you want for your own good or the good of humanity. No one else can come into this place unless you invite them. This is where you will come to meditate, visualize, practice skills, and seek healing in the future. Now let's begin to construct your mind gym in this space.

The mind gym can look any way you want to imagine it. My mind gym is on a mountainside, has a wooden floor but no ceiling, a space to train in yoga and hand-to-hand combat, and a seated mat for meditating. It looks somewhat like a yoga studio or a martial arts dojo. Now build yours. Does it have windows, or is it open to the sky? Are the floors wood or carpeted? What colors or types of artwork decorate the walls? What equipment do you need? Leave one wall blank to use as a screen for mental projection work. Otherwise, fill this gym with whatever you might need to practice in your mind and whatever brings you a sense of peace. Today, this first visit, all you need to do is build the space.

When you're finished and satisfied with your work, express gratitude for this gift of a safe, pristine place to train. Now leave your mind gym and make your way back to the doorway. Look back and review your handiwork. When you're ready, turn and step through the door, and then climb the steps back up to your outer conscious self, one at a time. Each step up brings you closer to your normal, wide-awake state. When you reach the top, follow the path back out into the active world, slowly bringing awareness to each part of your body. You will feel alert and energized as you open your eyes to end the exercise.

KISS (Keep It Simple, Smarty)

Fewer distractions and undivided resources equals stronger front-sight focus and better results, so "keep it simple, smarty." This tool is taught everywhere from elementary schools to business retreats because it works! Here's the WOS application.

Step 1: Begin by decluttering your daily spaces, working your way from small (your desk) to big (your garage). You don't have to do it all at once—tackle just one corner a day.

Step 2: Next, analyze your unique offer as described on page 47 and start parsing your daily tasks to identify your key 20 percent. For one week, record everything you do in 30-minute blocks, from Facebook time and commuting to working, training, even sleeping. Go deeper and record how you're spending time within those blocks. For example, while at work, are you checking e-mail twice a day or every ten minutes? At the end of the week, analyze and chunk it down to get a picture of what you're really doing every day. Now that you know, you can weed out those actions or time-sucks that aren't serving you so you can focus on producing the results you want.

Step 3: Finally, it's time to clear out your internal junk by eliminating unwanted or otherwise distracting obligations, grudges, past grievances, negative beliefs, and unfinished emotional business. Anticipate and accept that there will be hard choices; seek to travel light internally and make a positive impact, otherwise treading softly on the world. This is the Way of the SEAL.

Following these three steps helps make simplicity a visceral experience. You can intellectualize something, but there's a certain point where you need to embody or experience a concept before you really understand it. That's why we start with clearing stuff out physically. If you faithfully perform all three steps, you can't help but get the power of KISS at a root level. And because KISS applies to everything you do, you'll be able to integrate the concept into all aspects of your life. Increasing your effectiveness by making things simpler is an unbeatable combination.

PRINCIPLE 3

BULLETPROOF YOUR MISSION

Begin with the end in mind.
—STEPHEN R. COVEY, BESTSELLING AUTHOR OF *THE SEVEN HABITS OF HIGHLY EFFECTIVE PEOPLE* (1932–2012)

There is a reason more than 95 percent of new business ventures fail within five years: Folks don't have the skills to eliminate uncertainty and mitigate risk. Though my SEAL experience should have taught me better, I didn't practice front-sight focus well when I launched the Coronado Brewing Company in partnership with my wife's brothers after I left active duty in late 1996.

The CBC was a beautiful, high-end brewery and restaurant in Coronado, California, home of the West Coast SEALs. Invited to partner in a small craft-brew taproom concept, I saw a bigger vision that I thought my partners saw, too, and soon found myself writing a plan for a much more audacious brewery restaurant business. The plan went into detail about the capital we would need, who would manage the business, the menu, and other things that, in retrospect, had little chance of turning out the way we imagined. I know now that to support front-sight focus, you must bulletproof your mission against failure.

Within my limited perspective, I was clear on the CBC mission: Launch and operate a successful brewpub. However, I failed to properly define this mission, overlooking implicit expectations that included such things as ensuring adequate capitalization (I did not), building a team of "A" players in sync with the mission (nope), and ensuring my targets were of high value and well selected (mine weren't).

At first I focused on the obvious targets, such as raising money, building the facility, hiring and training the staff, and getting through the regulatory process. However, as we got closer to launch, my focus shifted to getting the doors open as fast as possible because we were running out of funds and I felt pressured to generate cash flow. Unfortunately, while I struggled to hit this survival target, I lost sight of my overall mission of building a solid business foundation capable of sprouting multiple operating units. I also lost sight of the targets critical to that mission's success, such as synchronizing our visions as a team (my vision included launching more brewpubs, but my partners had no interest in expansion), developing effective communications and trust (we did not have any brutally honest conversations, which you will learn the importance of in "Training in the Way of the SEAL"), or refining the systems of financial controls and operations so our business could grow (which required a skill set completely different from my own).

As I threw my heart into the venture, aiming for the short-term targets I could easily see, the higher-value targets I had neglected and the implicit expectations of running such a business overwhelmed me. Though we did open the doors within nine months of receiving our SBA loan and breaking ground, drawing a growing base of loyal customers, the partnership faltered quickly when challenges surfaced.

To make matters worse, I failed to prepare myself mentally and emotionally for the roller coaster of family dynamics that ensued, sweeping both my wife and her parents into the drama. Though looking back I am proud of what I built—a thriving business to this day— I deeply regret that its creation tore my wife's family apart as they argued about my loyalty to the investors over my brothers-in-law, and my father-in-law's loyalty to me over his sons. The disparity in visions and my failure to bulletproof the mission certainly contributed to the fallout. I did plenty of envisioning, but since the goal itself was misaligned with our reality, the mental work I did failed to deliver the desired results.

I recognize in hindsight that without proper planning and refined execution strategies, my entrepreneurial adventure was a gamble filled with hope and expectation, but no certainty. To avoid my costly mistakes, you must bulletproof your mission, which means:

- selecting only high-value targets
- exploring your options
- communicating your vision to others
- dirt-diving the mission

With the CBC, we failed to put many of these aspects into place as a team, which, as you have learned, soon led to serious breakdowns between my partners and me. After they reneged on their commitment to invest side-by-side with me or actually work in the business daily, and as I began to realize our sense of ethics was not the same, we split into warring factions. I found myself embroiled in a legal battle for control of the business and a family nightmare to boot. A pending sale of the restaurant fell through when the suitor learned of the mess. The three-year ordeal had severe consequences for my wife's family—her two brothers (my partners) became estranged from her, and her parents split up, allegedly from the stress.

Throughout this period, I focused on helping Sandy get through everything with as little collateral damage as possible while preserving our marriage, and on doing right by the shareholders. After all, it was they who risked the money and invested, along with me, in my vision of a larger business organization. Ultimately, I was able to return their capital with a profit, but it was an ugly few years, to say the least. It took me several more years to understand the full scope of what went wrong and to find the silver lining. I vowed never to make those same mistakes again, and to this day I am wary of partners and investors (though I might add that Sandy and my stepdaughters are all working for SEALFIT, and we get along quite well). This painful experience enlightened me in many ways, and I'm grateful for the lessons. I'm also grateful to my partners for being my teachers, though I admit it took a long time to find that gratitude. Hindsight is 20/20, and I can see clearly now how I could have bulletproofed the CBC mission to succeed at a high level. Let's look at the four principles introduced above in detail so that your missions will have a better outcome every time.

Select High-Value Targets

Success doesn't come to you ... you go to it.

—MARVA COLLINS, AMERICAN EDUCATOR AND FOUNDER OF WESTSIDE PREPARATORY SCHOOL (1936–)

Choosing the right targets from the outset helps bulletproof your mission because you'll know exactly where your resources are best directed. This supports your ability to ignore or delegate distractions that occur along the way and remain front-sight focused, which in turn significantly improves your chances of success. If I'd used a better planning process, I would have chosen more precise targets for CBC to ensure a healthier business beyond opening the doors and maintaining a positive daily balance in our bank account. I've since developed and tested one.

A simplified version of the target analysis process used by the SEALs, this powerful process ensures that the target "FITS" the mission and keeps you from tackling the wrong targets. You may be familiar with the business analysis tool called SWOT (Strengths, Weaknesses, Opportunities, Threats). The SWOT analysis helps you evaluate your strengths and weaknesses as compared to your competitors' with the intent of choosing a mission in the context of the marketplace. The FITS (Fit, Importance, Timing, Simplicity) process has some similarities, but I specifically designed it to determine which

targets best fit the mission you've chosen, which in turn should connect to your purpose as discussed with Principle 1. If you are already
familiar with SWOT and find it useful, you can easily combine it with
the FITS process for a one-two knockout punch.

In the Exercises section, I'll walk you through how to apply the
FITS process as you create your mission plan. Briefly, FITS asks you
to look at each possible target with regard to four criteria:

- Does this target **fit** your skills and your team and does it
  give you a good return on your investment?
- How **important** is this target to achieving mission success?
- Is the **timing** optimal for pursuing this target?
- Is the target **simple** and clear?

You can use this process to evaluate a preselected target or assign
each target under consideration a score from 1 to 5 in each of the four
categories. When you tally up the numbers, you'll know which targets
are higher value.

For example, my original partner in the CBC, Rick, initially suggested we open a taproom. After analysis of the ROI, opportunity
cost for my time, and the talent we had with a master brewer friend, I
pushed for the more ambitious and fitting target of a brewpub where
we would make and sell the beer with a full food menu. Because I saw
our mission as building a sustainable retail business that offered radical growth opportunities—and not just one shop—a brewpub struck
me as a better opportunity for franchising than a taproom.

I was right about the ROI potential of the brewpub. Ultimately,
though, it became clear that Rick (and his brother, who came on as
a partner later) did not share my vision of the overall mission, so this
target did not fit our team.

After we'd decided to pursue the brewpub concept, I found
myself neck-deep and drowning in the effort to launch the CBC.
In that moment, my short-term target of opening early to get some
cash flow *seemed* important because of our critical financial situation.
However, this situation arose only because I failed to focus on the

more important target earlier in the game: If I had raised the right amount of capital out of the gate, I could have remained front-sight focused on higher-value targets later.

A key criterion for FITS is timing, and our timing was excellent. Early to the microbrewery market, we saw an opportunity to be both the first brewpub in our town and a destination restaurant in an area with a ton of residents and no upscale eating establishments. We were able to fix on a location and were well ahead of the competition. This is one of the reasons the business was so successful in spite of our structural and team dysfunctions! Unfortunately, while the goal of launching a brewpub chain was very clear, the implicit tasks involved made the execution of this goal anything but simple. Our team had neither the experience to build a multiunit restaurant chain nor the cohesiveness to achieve that mission without major restructuring.

Though the FITS process generally would have supported me in pushing for the brewpub over a taproom, it also would have helped me identify major flaws in the plan early on, especially regarding the perceived simplicity of achieving the target. And had I continued to apply it as I aimed for each successive target on the way to building the CBC—from concept to launch—I would certainly have maintained a better front-sight focus on the right, high-value targets instead of allowing myself to get distracted when I felt pressure.

It takes discipline to focus only on high-value targets instead of giving in to the temptation of the low-hanging fruit life serves up daily. While serving the fledgling CBC as CEO, I had the opportunity to acquire another brewery in San Diego. The owner was already our master brewer for CBC, and I thought it would be a nice vehicle for expansion. I executed the deal, but unfortunately the time wasn't right and we didn't have enough cash to achieve my vision for expansion. Sometime after I sold my interest in the venture, it was offloaded to another entrepreneur. Again, if I had followed the FITS process, I would have realized I should have skipped this acquisition and instead spent my time and energy on raising adequate funding, facilitating better communications with my partners, and preparing our marketing and operating systems for expansion.

Explore Your Options

*When it's obvious that a goal cannot be reached, don't adjust the
goal, adjust the action steps.*
—CHINESE PROVERB

The right path forward is rarely crystal clear. Often we have multiple options for satisfying our goals, but they won't rank equally as best for your situation. The key is to scope out your options so you can make the strongest decision for ensuring mission success. Doing so will help you determine the optimum path forward, the details of which ultimately become your mission plan. But how do you identify and analyze your options in a way that bulletproofs your mission?

During a mission to Iraq in 2004 as part of a one-year Reserve call-up, I observed a special Marine detachment in order to analyze whether the Marines could fit within the U.S. Special Operations Command (better known as USSOCOM, a command overseeing the Special Forces components of the Army, Air Force, Navy, and Marine Corps), or whether their special units should continue to support only Marine Corps missions. The data I compiled was parsed, analyzed, and used to develop recommendations on courses of action to the Secretary of Defense. The Military Decision Making Process (MDMP) we used is designed for organizations with large staffs and a lot of time on their hands, as it requires many hours of labor. Nevertheless, it is such a great tool that I've created a simplified version more appropriate for rapid business environments.

Once you've selected your high-value targets, you will use the PROP process to explore your options for achieving them and zero in on the right path forward. This tool asks:

- What are your current **priorities**?
- What are the **realities** of the situation?
- What **options** do your targets suggest?
- Which **path** forward will you select?

In 2007, when my business, U.S. Tactical, lost a $5 million SEAL-candidate mentoring contract to Blackwater USA under sketchy circumstances, my priorities completely shifted. I identified my highest-value targets as damage control (basically tying up loose ends with my staff for the most positive outcome) and deciding my next step now that my primary business mission had unexpectedly derailed. The priorities I identified as related to these targets were ensuring that I treated my staff fairly, determining whether to contest the decision, and deciding if I wanted to stay in the government-contracting business or shift focus to the consumer market.

As I considered the situation, I came to terms with a few realities: The ten-ton gorilla of Blackwater vastly outgunned U.S. Tactical, a relative newcomer on the contracting scene, in both resources and experience. Going head to head with them by contesting the decision probably wouldn't end well for me, and even if I won, the effort could cost us the goodwill of our former employers or even bankrupt my company. Moreover, I wanted to take care of my employees, all former Navy Special Operators. They wouldn't earn a paycheck while I fought my way through the bureaucratic red tape, but taking care of them didn't necessarily mean keeping them with U.S. Tactical; Blackwater recognized the value of their experience and wanted to absorb them. I had a short window in which to decide my next move.

Based on these realities, I identified three options for achieving my target of damage control, which likewise affected my need to decide my next move: to hold my employees to their noncompete contracts and press on in a dispute with the Navy, to release them so they could seek a role with Blackwater while I pursued an entirely new business concept, or to retain them and seek a partnership with the new firm. I ultimately selected option two, which seemed the noblest decision since it was best for my employees and the would-be heroes they served; was in alignment with my stand (in particular: "My peace and happiness will be found in seeking truth, wisdom, and love, and not by chasing thrills, wealth, titles, or fame"); and freed me up to pursue my true passion of developing a new integral training model, something the Navy's guidelines for SEAL candidates hadn't fully allowed.

This process led me to the right decision, as the seed of SEALFIT grew out of the space created when I turned away from U.S. Tactical and the convoluted world of government contracting. The other options may have appeared warranted or more lucrative, but neither was in alignment with my vision any longer. Thankfully, I reoriented to get on track with my purpose, which at that point had evolved post-SEALs to facilitating personal transformation through integral training inspired by history's great warrior traditions.

Again, I will show you exactly how to apply the PROP process to your mission planning in the Exercises section.

Communicate the Mission

You have to see the pattern, understand the order,
and experience the vision.
—MICHAEL E. GERBER, BESTSELLING AUTHOR
OF *THE E-MYTH REVISITED* (1936–)

If you can't communicate your mission, you won't get support, and worse, you may not recognize disparities between your vision and your stakeholders'. Both of these factors are potential chinks in your mission's armor. You want people—whether they are potential partners, investors, or holders of other support roles—to understand clearly what you want to do, why you're doing it, what resources are required, and who's in charge. In the SEALs, I learned to do this by telling a story. The process of framing your mission as a story creates a visual mosaic of the mission plan, which is easy to digest for the team and others who need to be in the know, such as logistical partners (think helicopters and submarines) and higher-up decision makers. Instead of a boring slide reading, "Alpha Platoon will be in vehicles one and two," we'd present a picture. You'd immediately see you're in the right front, driving vehicle number two. Then you'd see the target shown with a picture from above, from an angle, the point of entry, and probably even a video of the surrounding area. For special operators, the visual mosaic is a critical part of our briefing process and includes the story of how we're going to get to the target, how we're going to take it down, and how we're going to exploit the on-site intelligence. When communicating a business mission, you'd tell the story of the business concept, the product(s), and the future as you see it unfolding. This third and final part of creating a bulletproof mission plan is framed by a tool I call SMACC (Situation, Mission, Action, Command, and Communication), which I'll walk you through in the Exercises section.

This is one of the things I actually did well with the CBC project (at least in terms of communicating to everyone besides my partners). I hired a graphic artist to render images of the envisioned brewpub inside and out and even design discount coupons and coasters. These images were inserted into my mission plan (read: business plan) with some text here and there to make my vision cohesive. I showed the presentation to bankers, family, friends, and anyone else I thought might have money to invest. I raised a million and a half dollars, $800,000 of it from my bank. Can you imagine a banker lending $800,000 to someone who had never managed a restaurant, brewed any beer, or even started a business before? Crazy, right? That's how effective visual storytelling can be.

The SEALs use a specific briefing process for this. The mission brief is where team leaders present the visual story of the mission to the team and higher-echelon leaders. They ensure that everyone sees their roles clearly, including what happens when things inevitably go wrong. Likewise, you must brief your team's mission until your teammates know their roles inside and out.

Our conscious mind represents a small fraction of our brainpower, while our subconscious dominates the rest—the part not easily reached by language, but by sensory impressions and images. If you limit communication to that word-oriented analytical mind, you're not going to inspire anybody. People didn't invest in the brewery because of my spreadsheets or simply for the return on investment. They invested because my vision was real to them: They wanted to go there and have a good time; they wanted to drink great beer with their friends in this incredibly warm environment with beautiful brick, wood-burning fireplaces, and brass kettles.

Dirt-Dive the Mission

The way to get started is to quit talking and begin doing.
—WALT DISNEY, AMERICAN ENTREPRENEUR AND FOUNDER OF THE
WALT DISNEY COMPANY (1901–1966)

Once you've clearly and visually defined your mission, you need to reconnect with it viscerally. Review it each morning individually and then review it together with your team in your weekly meetings.

In the Teams, after we were briefed, we'd go out and do a "dirt-dive," which is a fancy way of saying we rehearsed until the team had won the mission in their minds. When the Joint Special Operations Command SEAL team located Osama bin Laden, they didn't just hop in a helicopter and go get him like in the movie *Zero Dark Thirty*—they dirt-dived their plan for months. They ran through it in their minds. They rehearsed it in a mock compound. They debriefed what went right and the potential screwups. The team could envision mission success in exquisite detail. So it was an easy day (SEAL-speak for just another mission) when it came time to hit the actual target.

Ideally, you will want to include both mental and physical components when you dirt-dive your mission. However, sometimes a physical rehearsal may not make sense or be possible. At minimum, it's always a good idea to dirt-dive through a "mental rehearsal," another type of visualization you can do in your mind gym. At Colgate University, I had an amazing swim coach, Bob Benson, an early pioneer of visualization for sports performance. Coach, as we called him, had me visualizing my 200-yard breaststroke race each night before bed while timing myself with a stopwatch. This was not an easy task. I often dozed off, or my thoughts wandered toward my girlfriend, after diving in and making a single lap. I almost turned in my mental swimsuit but Coach encouraged me to keep visualizing.

I stuck with the training and after three months I could usually muddle through eight imagined lengths. After six months, I was consistently able to complete all eight lengths of the race in my mind. My confidence grew, but I never got to test the project because I took the fall semester in London. I hadn't trained or raced in months when I was invited to the spring championships the following year, yet I flew off the blocks with a surge of energy. Despite being out of practice, my stroke had gained a new smoothness. As I touched the wall and looked up at my time, I was stunned. I'd finished with my best time ever—the same time I had clocked in my visualization sessions a year earlier!

Dirt diving isn't just for SEALs and athletes, either. Lawyers, for example, will rehearse questions with witnesses before calling them to the stand during trial, playing both themselves and opposing counsel so the witnesses know what to expect (and so the lawyers can anticipate weak spots in the testimonies). I find this practice less prevalent in business than it should be, however. A WOS leader can dirt-dive board meetings, product launches, and new operating plans with their teams before going live. When you and your team connect with a mission regularly, when you work out all the kinks and anticipate all the potential problems, your familiarization will enable you to face the real thing as if it were just another day.

★ ★ ★ EXERCISES ★ ★ ★

CREATE A BULLETPROOF MISSION PLAN

In this exercise, you will work through a mock mission plan related to either your business or personal life—for example, to launch a new product, service, or venue, or to lose weight.

Part 1: Select a Target that FITS

Use the FITS process (Fit, Importance, Timing, and Simplicity) to analyze your potential targets (which should all be SMART goals, as we'll discuss under Principle 5) and narrow the choices down to the most high-value targets so you can map out an effective mission plan. You can use the guidelines provided to evaluate a preselected target, or you can use a simple 1 to 5 ranking system for each category to help determine which target out of several is optimal. The latter approach would serve well as an opportunity analysis tool to rank new business or project possibilities.

- **Fit.** Does the target you're considering fit your team? Is it the best use of talent, time, and energy? What will it cost to engage this target, and does the return on investment (ROI) make it worth the effort?

- **Importance.** How important is the target to your broader strategic mission? What effect will mission accomplishment have on you? On your competitors?

- **Timing.** Is the timing right to go after this target? Are you too early or too late? Are you ready? Can you find and reach the target, and how is the competition going to respond when you reach it?

- **Simplicity.** Is the target simple and clear? Is it something you can achieve without degrading your reputation, future capacities, or team cohesiveness?

Part 2: PROP Up Your Actions

Armed with your selected high-value target(s), use the PROP system (Priorities, Realities, Options, and Path) to develop at least three courses of action and choose one clear path forward.

- **Priorities.** Of your high-value targets, determine and prioritize your top three or four for mission success. Are there any other priorities related to achieving your top high-value targets?

- **Realities.** Get clear about the realities of your current situation and the influence these have on your targets and overall mission. How do these aspects affect your ability to satisfy your priorities?

- **Options.** Based on your evaluation of your priorities and situation, develop and rank up to three options or courses of action for achieving your top high-value targets and, ultimately, your mission. Often you'll end up combining elements from two or all three options in the final plan. (Note: You can use a creativity-building exercise like the one below to help support this step.)

- **Path.** Which course of action is the best fit? This is your path, along which you will develop your plan for hitting each target on the way to overall mission success.

Part 3: SMACC Down Your Mission

Decide on an initial course of action from Part 2 and create the visual mosaic or "story" you will use to communicate the mission to others. You can frame your story with a process I call SMACC:

- **Situation.** What are the background circumstances leading to a need for action? Why is it that the target

FITS the team right here and now? You must envision and research every detail so everyone can understand the backdrop to your mission.

- **Mission.** What exactly is the mission? Write a statement using SMART terminology (Specific, Measurable, Achievable, Realistic, and Timely or Time-Bound—see Principle 5 for more on this). Make sure you include your targets and use words that conjure images in your audience's mind.

- **Action.** What actions will your operating team perform? What about your administrative and logistical support teams? Actions are the meat and potatoes of your plan. No plan survives contact with the enemy—meaning that reality often requires adjustments—so make sure you include contingencies for when things go wrong.

- **Command.** Who's in charge of what and when? This is important, since leadership roles will likely shift during the mission. Plan contingencies for this part as well.

- **Communication.** How will teammates communicate with each other and to others? Who will communicate which messages in what timeframe, using what methods?

Use visual terms and avoid jargon; for example, say "It'll be dark as heck" instead of "The illumination will be at 10 percent due to a waning moon." Use pictures and videos to tell your story as I did when seeking investors for the CBC. Have your team visualize completing the mission at each stage, and then rehearse it physically and/or mentally as appropriate to the mission.

THE IDEA LAB

Bulletproofing your mission against failure in part depends on ensuring you've chosen your targets wisely. Before you can use the tools in this chapter to assess your options, you need to become aware of what they are! This exercise is essentially a WOS approach to brainstorming that can be just as effective at the individual level as with a team.

When you're considering your options for pursuing a target, for example, begin by putting on your "Morale Officer" hat and ensure you are in a positive, playful, and creative state of mind. In your journal, articulate your challenge clearly, drawing pictures if possible to tap into the powers of your subconscious.

Now, stop thinking. Sit in silence with your eyes closed, letting your mind settle. Visit your mind gym following the usual meditation as outlined on page 54. When you get there, you will use it as an idea lab by bringing your attention back to the challenge or question as you've articulated it and just watch the projection screen and wait for a response. You'll want to record whatever comes up, so to avoid interrupting your flow, consider having a mini-recorder handy, or let someone you trust write down your thoughts for you as you speak them aloud. It's important that you remember (or ask your partner to remind you) not to fall back on actively thinking about a solution; rather, let your mind remain blank and clear. Record anything that rises into your consciousness or appears on your projection screen, whether it is a word, a fully formed thought, a feeling, or an image.

After five or ten minutes, transfer your ideas and impressions onto sticky notes, which you will post up on a wall or board (or simply use your journal). Now, review your collection of notes and see what connections or further thoughts spring to mind. First impressions are typically closest to the mark, no matter how odd they may seem, so refrain from judging yours. Anything goes.

If you're doing this exercise with a team, the instructions are essentially the same. State the challenge out loud so everyone is on the same page, then have each participant visit their mind gym or just sit silently if they aren't familiar with the mind gym practice. Everyone should speak their ideas, images, and impressions out loud while one person records these on sticky notes as described. Remember, anything goes, so no judging or teasing each other while you review the results.

PRINCIPLE 4

DO TODAY
WHAT OTHERS WON'T

Do today what others won't; do tomorrow what others can't.

—SMOKE JUMPER CREED

Anyone familiar with the SEALs has heard of Hell Week, a grueling period of what some might call torture. Training goes on 24 hours a day for six days, and instructors allow you a total of four hours' sleep during the week. You're freezing most of the time between the cold night air and the even colder ocean water. Most quit between Sunday, when Hell Week begins, and Tuesday night, typically just a couple hours shy of dawn when they are feeling most vulnerable and exhausted. However, by the time Wednesday rolls around, when you're so fatigued you start hallucinating, your body does a strange thing. After four days of breaking down from the lack of sleep and all the physical training, it starts adapting. You start getting stronger.

Many folks go their whole lives without transcending the sense of self and world they settle into as adults. The SEALs figured out how to do it in a week. Though I won't ask you to forego sleep while you run intense drills, in this chapter I will push you to:

- find your 20X factor
- embrace the suck
- build the Three Ds (discipline, drive, and determination)

To become the best version of yourself possible, you must suck it up and do the work! So here we go.

Find Your 20X Factor

To dare is to lose one's footing momentarily.
To not dare is to lose oneself.
—SOREN KIERKEGAARD, DANISH PHILOSOPHER
AND THEOLOGIAN (1813–1855)

"You guys are capable of at least twenty times what you think you are. Now get off your sorry asses and hit the surf!" Lieutenant Zinke yelled into his bullhorn as we jumped and ran back to the surf zone for the umpteenth time. It was Tuesday night of Hell Week. As we locked arms in the zone, Zinke shouted, "Take seats!" We sat arms locked, backs to the surf. Buffeted by the water, shivering uncontrollably, we held each other close in the hopes some warmth would transfer. Someone began to sing the national anthem, which raised our spirits a bit. I set my sights on just getting through this evolution (the term the SEALs use for training events). I couldn't think beyond that or I'd be too overwhelmed to continue. "One at a time," I thought. "I can do this, piece of cake."

"Man, this sucks!" my swim buddy Swanson said through gritted teeth.

"Just breathe deeply and visualize yourself on the beach in Hawaii," I joked. That's what I was doing, and it sure made me feel better, even if I was kidding myself.

Swanson and I made it through the night, but the class lost another ten trainees. As Thursday rolled in, there were about thirty of us left with two plus days to go. Though my exhausted, sleep-deprived mind craved rest, I began to notice my body getting stronger. *Maybe I really am capable of twenty times more than I think I am. What are my limits?* I wondered. I'm still wondering to this day, as I have repeatedly blown past my own expectations and seen thousands of others do the same.

The SEALs aren't the first band of warriors to figure out the "20X factor." Ancient forms of yoga, which prepared warriors for battle, required *tapas,* translated as a "mighty effort." This effort was put forth in long-term, rigorous training lasting hours a day, and through extremely difficult poses that took years to perfect. The yoga training also integrated difficult breathing exercises and sustained periods of meditation to shed weakness and sharpen the mind. The ancient Spartans used the agoge, a brutal training program for young warriors that forged mental and physical toughness. The Eastern martial arts, such as those of the Shaolin monks and ninjutsu, and native warriors such as the Apache scouts all embraced the 20X factor as well.

You may think that progress in science and material wealth means we don't have to suffer the challenges these warriors endured. That would be missing the point—hard work built character then as it does now, while a soft life weakens it. Comfort imprisons us in a low-grade fear of suffering. We naturally shy from things that hurt, not understanding how much this pattern debilitates us and keeps us from experiencing life at its fullest. We must define our comfort zone, and then get the heck out of it! The 20X factor is all about embracing a personal culture of mighty effort.

You can experience growth through challenges of a less physical or even nonphysical nature, too. Try a yoga challenge where you do a class every day for sixty days. If you have more time, you could travel to an unknown culture and immerse yourself without speaking English, or go for that advanced degree you've been putting off. The more adventurous might try jumping out of a perfectly good airplane or training for an obstacle race. None of these requires you to be a premier athlete; the point is to do anything that breaks your cycle of disempowering behavior and builds your mental toughness muscles. Through this mighty effort, you'll cross your first 20X threshold, which will bring you to an entirely new level of personal power.

It can be scary to take on a new challenge, and your fears can get in the way. Once, I took a group of executives on a challenge trip to New Mexico. During the last evolution of the day, which was a 100-foot rappel off a cliff overlooking the Rio Grande, I discovered one executive had an extreme fear of heights. "Ed, just focus on your breathing and take it one step at a time," I told him. Skeptically, he lowered down the rock face, then panicked and flipped upside down. Though he wasn't in any real danger, fear overwhelmed him, and he began screaming for help. It took every ounce of self-restraint to stop from rescuing him, but I knew the only way for him to learn from this situation was for him to right himself.

I shouted to Ed, "Stop screaming! Focus and get control of yourself. Breathe deeply and close your eyes." My words shocked him into a focused state. He did as I instructed and started to regain control. "Now hold onto the rope, get your feet onto the wall, and push off," I coached from below, praying he could maintain his composure and avoid hurting himself unnecessarily. I had never felt out on a limb like this during a training event and I understood the risks to my business if something went wrong. If this exercise left Ed injured—even if that was his own doing—it would kill my reputation. He could even sue me. Fortunately, I was able to help Ed realize that he was the master of his own fate; he finally followed my instructions, righting himself easily. I lowered him the rest of the way down and gave him a big hug.

On the ground and glad to be alive, Ed was euphoric but still a bit in shock. I understood that he was very receptive to learning, so I drove home the lesson of the 20X challenge and praised his efforts to face his fear, take control, and break through. Later at the dinner celebration, we all toasted his accomplishment. I never saw Ed again, but a year later I followed up with the team leader who hired me for the job. He told me Ed had lost a lot of weight, gotten into better physical shape, and was much more confident at work. His boss had even promoted him. His story, that of the executive who nearly fell into the Rio Grande, was now legendary in the company. He'd found his 20X factor and rewritten the story of the executive who was afraid of heights.

No Way Out But In

Are you an extra in someone else's play, or are you the author of your own drama? The reality of your present awareness is born from the intersection of your subjective story, which defines your sense of self, and your objective reality, which affects your behavior. You want your subjective story supported by purpose and strong values. You want to have integrity and great personal power. To ensure all that, you must become both the author and star of your own story, with events in your objective reality serving as opportunities to grow and connect.

However, too many of us succumb to a weak internal story informed by flawed but popular beliefs. We are reactionary to objective events, easily buffeted by the winds of change. Pop culture, people we interact with daily, and external events shape and reinforce this subjective reality. In these instances, we end up being extras in someone else's story, reacting our way through life, lacking integrity and out of balance.

I often meet individuals who appear squared away and successful by all society's measures, but are missing something and ready to do more work on the inside. Joe, for example, despite being a top performer in his industry and a good-looking, friendly guy, suffered from a fragmented internal sense of self that caused him much angst in his personal life. When I met him, he was emerging from a series of unsatisfying, shallow relationships. Most comfortable with his mastery of business, he was quick to steer conversation in that direction, making it hard to connect with him authentically.

When Joe first joined my training center, he shared with me that he had experienced trauma as a child living with his emotionally abusive, alcoholic mother. This left him unsettled, unfulfilled, and eager to leave that story behind. Joe had done hundreds of hours of personal development and therapy, but at age fifty-four still sought a way to feel more valuable and whole. One day, he observed a Kokoro Camp, SEALFIT's fifty-hour civilian Hell Week training event. Joe's spirit stirred—he told me he wanted me to mentor him, to take him to the precipice through this crucible experience—yet he immediately came up with reasons for why he couldn't do it.

Deep down, I think Joe understood the need to challenge himself in this way and to confront his beliefs at a level beyond the intellectual, but wasn't sure exactly why he should do so, nor was he certain of his bigger purpose or his "why." Reverting to what he knew best, he initially approached me with the intention of joining the program and filming his progress to create a product out of the experience. It was clear to me that he needed to do this work for deep transformation, not for a quasi-business reason, so I said no. He then asked me if I thought he had what it took to get through SEALFIT Academy (our three-week program, which many people take as a buildup to Kokoro Camp) and Kokoro Camp. "Joe, only you would know!" I replied. Finally, he asked what would be the biggest benefit of committing to the program. I said, "Joe, within you is the voice of your true self. You can continue through life upgrading the story you've been given or you can write a new story. If you dare, you will meet yourself for the first time."

He accepted the challenge, capping off the three-week odyssey of the SEALFIT Academy with fifty hours of nonstop training in Kokoro Camp. It completely transformed him. My staff and I exposed Joe to physical, mental, and emotional challenges including arduous workouts, team challenges (such as "log PT," which pits a team of five against a 350-pound log held overhead), and long periods of meditation. Training commenced at 6 a.m. and ran until 8 p.m. daily. By taking him way beyond his comfort zone using the full spectrum of the training found in this book, we forced him to confront his most deeply held beliefs and face his subconscious programming. Joe quickly realized that he could safely discard much of the garbage cluttering his mind and heart, such as the faulty belief system regulating his self-esteem at that deep childhood level. Discovering his 20X factor not only removed his fear that others wouldn't accept the real Joe, but it also opened the doors to mental and emotional resources he didn't even know he had.

Joe kept training with us after completing Kokoro Camp, and we accepted him warmly as a teammate. He now sees himself more clearly, allowing himself to have more fun and intimacy in his romantic relationships and to move beyond a one-dimensional focus on business and wealth accumulation. Interestingly, his breakthrough has also allowed Joe's business to grow significantly. He found he could focus with even more precision on how to best serve his clients, which led to a reorientation of his business to help real estate professionals become healthier and happier while still providing them with tools for excellence in their profession. For personal fulfillment, he's started pursuing an advanced degree in spiritual psychology, a subject that excites his passion. "I finally found my voice," he told me, which helped him chronicle his transformation in a self-published book, *Willing Warrior*.

Most people shy from challenges of an extreme nature, and that's understandable given the level of comfort and wealth we're used to in Western society. As Joe will tell you, this is a big mistake. The keys to satisfaction, excitement, joy, and more lie on the other side of a great challenge. The industrial age brought material prosperity that eliminated a lot of the natural challenges life used to deliver—but it also brought obesity, poor health, lack of purposeful existence, and a general malaise with an alarmingly large percentage of the population in dependency. New stories and models of thinking are required to rebalance us. I'm not proposing we all become Spartans or Navy SEALs; rather, that we transcend the status quo to create a new cultural story and shatter the myth that easy is good and hard is bad. What qualifies as "hard" occurs on a spectrum that will be different for everyone based on your circumstances—the point is to push your limits and acknowledge this mighty effort as both positive and necessary for true happiness.

Embrace the Suck

I am just an average man, but by God
I work harder than the average man.
—WINSTON CHURCHILL, BRITISH PRIME MINISTER (1874–1965)

SEAL trainers often say, "Pain is weakness leaving the body." This encouraging metaphor describes a fascinating alchemy: the transmutation of training-induced pain into confidence when performing, whether on the battlefield, playing field, or in life. Another famous saying in the Teams, used when the going gets tough, is "Suck it up!" So, as I did during Hell Week, you can "embrace the suck" of temporary pain to develop a can-do attitude and lean into any hard task without wavering or whining. You don't have to be a superman or superwoman. You just have to endure pain better than the average man or woman.

Whether we're talking about mental or physical effort, the first step to embracing the suck is to step up and face your fear of suffering. We all share this fear, which stems from a deep-rooted need for certainty and security. Pain is your body's way of telling you that security is threatened because something is out of whack. However, when you consistently experience the personal growth that accrues from deliberately putting yourself out of balance, such as with hard workouts, you begin to embrace that temporary pain for the rewards it brings. The fear recedes into oblivion as you embrace the suck. Each time the instructors at BUDS pushed me beyond where I thought I could go, the pain at first caused a sensation of fear, which I transformed into focused determination. After my mind and body regained balance (and I noted that I wasn't disabled), the experience made me stronger and wiser. There was nothing to fear from the pain but the fear itself. This happened repeatedly during my time in the SEALs, and it has become a habit since.

It is important to understand the difference between good pain and bad pain so that you'll know when to push through and when to dial it down. One of my mentors, Ashtanga yoga authority Tim Miller, likes to call good pain "integrating pain" and bad pain "dis-integrating pain." Good pain—whether physical or emotional—is associated with growth and makes you stronger. Think of exercise-induced pain, for instance, or the pain of making the kind of hard choices necessary for maintaining front-sight focus on your goals. Bad pain, on the other hand, is the kind that hurts you physically or emotionally and is associated with injury or regret, things that stop you in your tracks or hold you back.

The fact is, we tend to avoid pain in all its forms, whether good or bad. I encourage you to continue avoiding dis-integrating pain. However, integrating pain is good for you—you must learn to lean into it. In reality, the depth and duration of integrating pain can be mentally controlled. By acknowledging the value you get from integrating pain and embracing it for this value over the long term, you will find the process becoming easier until you eventually enjoy the pain for the type of person it is forging you into. If you dwell on the pain itself, it gets more intense, lasts longer, and can cause you to quit and avoid it in the future. The secret is to acknowledge the pain and then immediately focus on something else, such as the positive benefits it brings. The pain will quickly diminish in volume and duration, freeing you to continue growing into the person and the life you most desire.

Focus on the Positive

One simple technique for embracing the suck of any painful situation is to change your state by immediately focusing on something else that is positive . . . and then smiling or even laughing. This worked wonders during SEAL training. Some of my funniest and fondest memories are of the most difficult events. Because I put on a happy face and found humor in some oddity of the moment, the pain disappeared, replaced by growing confidence and courage. On Thursday of Hell Week, for example, one of the instructors caught me joking with another student. He took it upon himself to try to break me then and there. "Divine, get your sorry ass over here!" he barked, his look enough to cool the waters off Waikiki. I made my way over to "Instructor Evil" and stood at attention, awaiting my sentencing. "I'm gonna make you quit, and I ain't gonna leave until you do," he said with a matter-of-fact smile. I smiled back at him, which he definitely didn't like. He smiled wider. "Let's start with one thousand eight-count body builders."

"Okay," I thought, "time to dig deep. He'll have to kill me to get me to quit, so I had better pass out doing these builders before I die." I dug into the exercises (a full body movement where you squat down and jump to a plank position, then hop your legs out wide and back, finally jumping forward to come to a standing position), counting each eight steps and the repetition number. After fifty reps, I was already smoked—I'd been awake and training around the clock since Sunday afternoon, nearly five days straight! By the time I got to four hundred, I was numb, but still moving. At seven hundred, I was physically and mentally done. Just like during my black belt test, I realized I needed to tap into my special weapons and get beyond the physical. In this case, I needed to find some humor in the moment to turn it positive, quick, so I just started laughing as if I'd heard the funniest joke ever. Instructor Evil turned his attention back to me and looked at me with an odd face. I kept moving and kept laughing, pretending I was in my own comedy show. Soon I was feeling 100 percent better, as if bolts of energy were flowing through me. I looked Instructor Evil in the eye and said, "Easy day, this is fun."

He smiled at me, genuinely this time, and said, "Get back with your class, Divine. Nice job." I realized later that showing inner strength was the whole point of his drill. He recognized me as one of the stronger officers in the class, but needed to see if I could handle his singling me out for the equivalent of a thousand burpees, especially when I thought there'd be more to come after I finished those. When he saw I was able to find my happy place and use humor to embrace the suck, he gave me my "get out of jail" card.

> ### WAY OF THE SEAL DRILL
> ....
> ## Transmuting Pain into Positivity
>
> As you tackle your next challenge, whether of the daily variety or a mighty effort, embrace the suck of the moment by shifting your focus to something positive, smiling, and even making yourself laugh. Take control of your story and use positive self-talk to reinforce your attitude adjustment. Connect the pain of the moment to your purpose and goals and know, deep inside, that you are traveling the upward spiral to success.
>
> In a group situation, take the next step and use these tools to help your teammates through a challenging moment. If someone has a look of pain or is otherwise expressing discomfort, encourage the person to smile. It may not look very convincing at first, but, after sticking with it, he or she will soon feel the positive psychological and physiological effects. Being strong for others can help you be strong for yourself as well, and it's incredibly empowering to find that you can change your story simply by taking control of your facial and verbal expressions. You may even find the situation becoming humorous or fun for real.

Go to the Challenge

A unique, if unfair, aspect of our beautiful human condition is that if you avoid challenge, it will come anyhow, bringing with it severe and painful lessons. The more you try to dodge them or insulate yourself through the trappings of wealth, emotional armor, or numbing agents like alcohol, the harder the challenges become. I recommend that you take yourself to the challenge instead of waiting for it to come to you as a way to burn off your lethargy in a controlled environment.

Though I've focused mostly on physical challenges in this chapter, any structured challenge will do the trick. If physical challenges scare you, take a good look at why. Don't let yourself off the hook too easily. To build your "embrace the suck" muscle, the key to your ability to do today what others won't, you *must* seriously challenge yourself. I'm not talking about challenging yourself to achieve goals you set for work; I'm suggesting you seek out gnarly challenges that may even seem unattainable. Recruiting your team to join you is a good way to develop accountability and momentum.

I can hear all of the "yeah buts" and "what ifs" as you read this:

- "Yeah, but I don't have the time or the fitness to do that."
- "What if I get injured?"
- "Yeah, but you are a Navy SEAL . . . easy for you to say."

These are all just excuses. Remember, what is hard for you may be easy for others—the key is to figure out what a "gnarly challenge" is for you and then go after it! Feeling resistance toward a big challenge is normal; pushing against resistance is the Way of the SEAL. For you, that might mean taking a short sabbatical to walk the Appalachian Trail with your son or daughter, or it might mean training to run a Spartan race with your work team. A friend told me about someone she knew who was having a terrible time with her teenage son. He was going down a bad road, using drugs and failing out of school. She tried intervening with therapy, but this didn't work, and as a single mom she struggled to deal with him while meeting the demands of earning a living. After trying many other traditional solutions and failing, she decided on a more radical approach—to sail around the world with him. Though he protested loudly, she dragged him kicking and screaming into the boat and together they navigated the seas for a year. The challenge and adventure changed their lives, opening both to new 20X horizons and bonding them in ways they could never have expected.

Structured challenges come in three forms. The first is a challenge requiring sustained long-term effort. This would include things such as a long-term commitment to five yoga sessions a week, to get a black belt in a martial art, or to master any challenging skill. Though getting an advanced degree also falls in this category, the most valuable challenges have a physical, mental, emotional, intuitional, and spiritual component.

Second are challenges that benchmark performance. There's a saying in business that if it's not measured, it's not real. A benchmark is a milestone measure that allows you to note and celebrate progress as a small victory in the larger context of your mission, and it's a great technique for building your ability to embrace the suck. When training for the CrossFit Games, I benchmarked my progress monthly with standardized workouts so I could track my strength, skill, and work capacity. Benchmarking keeps you focused, builds confidence, and removes doubt: When you arrive at the "big day," you will already know you can kick ass and take names.

The concept of benchmarking is well known in business. As the interim CEO of the software company Inasoft, my mission was to bridge the company from start-up to a venture capital–financed, growing company. After selling my interest in the Coronado Brewing Company, I took on this new role with a determination to be front-sight focused on my mission, so I set a series of clear targets that would also serve as benchmarks of my performance:

1. Secure beta tests of our software with five major companies and receive their endorsement.
2. Practice the pitch with twenty private investors and with local business partners.
3. Complete the arduous Southern California Tech Coast Angel funding process.
4. Secure funding from a Silicon Valley venture capitalist.

By the time we finished No. 3, we'd developed the credibility, confidence, and momentum to attract a big-money VC to the tune of $4 million. This concept is equally valid to benchmark your personal development. If you don't track your progress, then how will you know you are on the right path or even growing at all? What benchmarks can you set for your physical development, mental toughness, and spiritual strength?

The third structured challenge type is a crucible experience such as Kokoro Camp, an expedition like a world sailing tour or a mountain ascent. These will happen less frequently, but you can prepare with incremental efforts. Many of my peers do a minor challenge quarterly, such as an obstacle race or long hike. Then they will schedule a major challenge once every eighteen months or so.

All three of these challenge types will forge mental and emotional resilience, develop confidence, and reduce your fear of pain. This all feeds your upward spiral, supporting you as you embrace the suck, which in turn powers your ability to do today what others won't and leads to powerful new stories about what is possible in your life.

Build the Three Ds (Discipline, Drive, and Determination)

We are what we repeatedly do.
Excellence then, is not an act, but a habit.
—ARISTOTLE, GREEK PHILOSOPHER
AND POLYMATH (384 BCE-322 BCE)

At six foot two inches and 220 pounds, to describe Big Dave as "fit" wouldn't do the word, or the man, justice. A former saturation diver and power lifter, he needed strength training twice a day to release the pain from his regular run-ins with the bends. The most impressive thing about Dave, though? His character. One day while we were prepping our dive gear at SEAL Team THREE, I asked Dave why he loved diving so much.

"I love the act of diving, but also the type of person it's made me," he said. "Diving requires total focus; one mistake and you're done. You've got to have the discipline for detailed planning and preparation. But you must also be driven to see new worlds and explore new technologies, and you must have the determination to work longer and harder than others." Two years later, Dave left this world when his heart gave out during one of his ten-hour dives up the San Diego coast, but the example he set of developing habits of excellence resonate within me still.

Making a Habit of Excellence

Our habits are the little actions we perform every moment, every day, in between the big actions that occur less frequently. Though many of these aren't necessarily bad habits, they may not be "excellence habits" either. If you want to perform at the top 0.1 percent in your chosen arena, you must draw on your tool kit for remaining front-sight focused and embracing the suck in order to make excellence a habit.

When it comes to habits, the best approach isn't to focus on eliminating unwanted behaviors but to replace them with new habits and drown the old out. This is true of replacing a nasty habit like smoking with a healthy habit like exercise, and it's just as true with replacing a character habit like laziness with a more useful one such as embracing the suck. Our habits define us: Solid character habits define a solid character. I'd like you to start putting your mind to developing the character habits of discipline, drive, and determination.

We can all grow through a disciplined approach to learning, training, and self-mastery. But we can grow even stronger by driving passionately and in a focused manner toward our targets, facing hard challenges, and never quitting when the going gets unfathomable. And, perhaps above all, we grow the most through quiet determination and perseverance, expressed through a commitment to doing today what others won't.

Discipline

Discipline is the spark that ignites the fire of a habit. Those fires must be lit daily, and discipline provides the original source energy. The word discipline literally means to be a disciple to a higher purpose.

Developing the discipline to train hard every day means you become a disciple—not to the training itself, not just to looking good or stroking your ego, but to the higher purpose of developing yourself fully as a human being and as a leader. To return to the start of this chapter, discipline begins with training the mind to reject discomfort and embrace the suck.

This kind of discipline isn't built or acquired overnight. It starts with baby steps. Just committing to a training regimen is a first step. Take things up a notch now by disciplining yourself to go the extra mile every day. Rather than just showing up and "doing your job," seek to learn everything you can about what others do in your team or office, what other roles people play in your industry, and how things work. Ask questions, look for learning opportunities such as trainings or even informal conversations, and read widely. If you don't know something, make an effort to find out. If you know a little, try to learn a little more. Never rest on your laurels. Remember, when extraordinary efforts become commonplace, extraordinary results follow.

Drive

Whereas discipline activates a habit, drive is the motivation behind your actions. A fiery passion for diving excellence drove Big Dave to improve on the SEALs' diving programs. My desire to fulfill my purpose of serving as an inspiration for others and facilitating personal and global transformation drives me to share these stories and practices with you. Drive is fueled by desire, belief, and expectation that we can achieve something extraordinary through our efforts. It feeds on discipline in that it becomes stronger as we commit ourselves at deeper levels to our pursuits.

How do we build drive? First, connect a major life interest to your purpose and define a mission around it. For example, as I just mentioned, sharing my training philosophy and practices with others connects directly to my purpose: to be an inspiration for others through my example and teaching, facilitating personal and global transformation in the process. Drive will help keep you front-sight focused and moving toward your next target as you pursue mission success. Daily journaling is a great practice for ensuring that your purpose is in the forefront of your mind as you make decisions along the way. "Does this action move me closer to or farther from my purpose?" is a good reflection question.

Drive provides a lifelong source of energy if focused on a passionate and worthy end. But be wary, because drive can have a dark side, too. When you're driven solely by "me" reasons and you confuse determination with stubbornness, you can easily lose sight of the "we" in your life, leaving your coworkers, family, or other teams wondering what happened to that nice man or woman they used to know. This kind of drive may cause you to work so much you never spend time with your kids or to take all the credit for a project's success. The type of drive that powers elite operators is a "me plus we" drive. It means you're driven to grow and learn new things in a way that benefits yourself and your team, and that is balanced with the needs of the organization. Big Dave was driven by his passion for diving excellence, but understood his labor of love meant nothing unless the team also benefited. Because of his drive, the SEALs gained new procedures for underwater missions. He pioneered improved navigation techniques and pushed the envelope by testing cutting-edge, often experimental dive rigs and other equipment, all of which helped the SEALs better meet their maritime missions. Not stopping there, he developed a three-week training course for SEALs to master the techniques of underwater navigation and ship attacks, a program the SEALs use to this day when faced with a combat diving mission.

Determination

If drive is the fuel that keeps you motivated, determination is the longview commitment to the mission. Big Dave was always the last out of the Team area every night. When everyone else is done for the day, the determined stay for an extra hour honing a skill, working on their gear, or studying something new. World-class performers aren't always the most naturally talented at their craft. They are, however, the hardest working and most determined to be the best they can be at what they do. They are the ones who will do today what others won't.

★ ★ ★ EXERCISES ★ ★ ★

BRING IT!

Bring the challenge to you. Whether you're tackling physical challenges like running a marathon or an emotional one like having a difficult conversation, you must be deliberate in your approach. I recommend pushing boundaries by structuring a minor challenge once per week—this could be something like just saying no to new obligations, or adding five minutes to your usual workout routine. Then choose a monthly or quarterly challenge that requires more significant effort and planning, such as an all-day hike or attending a retreat that makes you uncomfortable (consider a silent or relationship-building retreat, each of which can be terror for many of us!). Cap it off with a good kick in the rear by choosing a gnarly challenge to tackle at least once a year.

FIND YOUR 20X FACTOR

Here are some ideas for your first 20X challenge. These may seem very difficult to accomplish—that's the point! However, you can scale them to your level of readiness. Typical disclaimers apply here—don't do anything dumb, and check with your doctor first. You can find other 20X challenge ideas at SEALFIT.com or come up with your own.

Gnarly Physical Challenges: If you consider yourself really fit, aim high with a bid for Everest, join SEALFIT Academy or Kokoro Camp, ride your bike across the country, hike the Appalachian Trail end to end, or attend the Boulder Outdoor Survival School. At home, try 1,000 push-ups or pull-ups for time (don't forget to benchmark your progress as you repeat over time).

Less Gnarly Physical Challenges: Take up an endurance or extreme sport. Beginner to intermediate athletes can look to a hot yoga challenge, joining a CrossFit gym, running a local marathon, or looking into our online SEALFIT and Unbeatable Mind programs. At home, try a one-mile walking lunge.

Mighty Nonphysical Effort: Volunteer for a church mission or a traveling service unit like the Red Cross, FEMA, or Doctors Without Borders. Find a way to work with disabled veterans—SEALFIT recently conducted a twelve-hour challenge pairing CEOs with newly disabled warriors. Conceived as a service to the vets, it turned out to be such a powerful and life-altering experience that it was a service to the CEOs and my staff as well. Perhaps you've met someone who uprooted and went to China to teach English . . . why not you? Or sign up for a weekend doing something that makes you deeply uncomfortable. There are many opportunities out there to shatter your paradigms and lead to growth.

FORGE MENTAL TOUGHNESS

Success seems to be largely a matter of hanging on
after others have let go.

—WILLIAM FEATHER, AMERICAN AUTHOR
AND PUBLISHER (1889–1981)

Making excellence a habit will take you a long way down the road toward every mission you focus on and enable you to satisfy your purpose, leading to a happier, more fulfilling, and meaningful life. But how exactly do you continue to hang on after others have let go? How do you just "not quit"? This is the million-dollar question—everyone who asks me wants a silver-bullet answer. Sorry, but there isn't one. You earn a nonquitting spirit in a trial-by-fire manner either through life challenges or through the kind of training I share with you in this book.

Interestingly, it's not necessarily the best athletes who succeed at BUDS. When psychologists studied what type of person makes it through SEAL training they could only agree it was those with "grit." I think of the Duke, John Wayne, in his best Western movie. Those who have grit are first in, last out, the hardest fighters who do it all with a smile on their faces. In SEAL-speak, "grit" means mental toughness. But how do you train to forge grit?

One of the first exercises I do with SEALFIT trainees is to have them take a push-up position and hold it for forty-five minutes. Of course, most of them fail after five minutes, but we get them back up again and again, prodding them with mental-toughness tactics. Ultimately, they amaze themselves and make it through the session. By holding them accountable to a standard they never thought attainable, they learn that their physical limits are actually determined by their mental limits. As I coach them through what is often their first 20X experience, I touch upon five fundamental skills they will use throughout the Academy and for the rest of their lives. Today, the SEALs teach four of these (arousal control, attention control, effective goal setting, and visualization) as the "Big 4" of mental toughness. I've added one more to the mix addressing the impact of our emotions on our inner strength—an often overlooked, but crucial factor, in our ability to forge grit. The five WOS skills for forging mental toughness are therefore:

- controlling your response
- controlling your attention
- developing emotional resilience
- setting effective goals
- visualizing powerfully

Control Your Response

Courage is grace under pressure.
—ERNEST HEMINGWAY, AMERICAN AUTHOR
AND JOURNALIST (1899–1961)

SEALs call it arousal control, but it's not what you may think: In the Teams, we're taught to use the breath as a method of inhibiting our physiological arousal or our "fight, flight, or freeze" response (previously known as "fight or flight"). The breath is the link between the sympathetic nervous system, which leads us into response mode, and the parasympathetic nervous systems, which brings us back into balance when the coast is clear. When triggered, the sympathetic nervous system pumps hormones such as cortisol, adrenaline, epinephrine, and norepinephrine into the bloodstream, causing immediate physical and psychological changes that ready the body for massive action against impending doom. However, without the skills to rebalance these systems at will, especially in a world where "doom" is often more metaphoric than true threat, it becomes a liability.

Your immediate and unconscious reaction to surviving such a moment, whether literally or figuratively, is likely to take a deep "phew" breath, followed by several more. Deep breathing is the universal shutoff switch to stress, but it's also useful proactively to maintain your focus, as we learned with Principle 2. Warriors have known this for centuries, making breathing practice central to their training—the ability to stay calm in battle or in a rescue operation creates the conditions necessary for courageous acts. Women understand it at an evolutionary level, almost automatically going into deep breathing patterns when giving birth (a more structured approach to this natural response makes up part of the Lamaze technique).

Breathing practice is an art mostly lost to the Western world, though it has found a few footholds. Research suggests that, today, most people use only a small percentage of their total lung capacity, leaving a lot of energy on the table. This is true in both aroused states and day-to-day moments. We've already explored how deep diaphragmatic breathing can help you calm yourself and help you prepare your mind for front-sight focus. But sometimes our breathing remains too shallow despite our best efforts. Especially in chaotic or very challenging situations, arousal control can feel like trying to slow a train rushing downhill, and that's assuming we remember to breathe deeply in the first place. To train arousal control and make deep breathing an automatic response, I teach a structured approach that I call Box Breathing.

Adding a Box Breathing exercise (found at the end of this chapter) to your daily training plan will help you defy statistics and reap big rewards. Box Breathing, when practiced daily, will fully oxygenize the blood with each breath, ensuring you have the fuel to work at optimal levels, while it detoxifies your lungs and internal organs. And, as with all deep-breathing exercises, it will calm and center your mind.

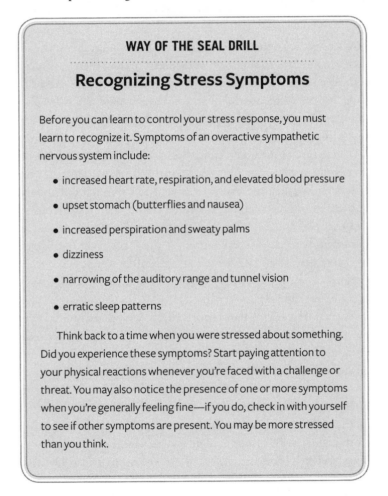

WAY OF THE SEAL DRILL

Recognizing Stress Symptoms

Before you can learn to control your stress response, you must learn to recognize it. Symptoms of an overactive sympathetic nervous system include:

- increased heart rate, respiration, and elevated blood pressure

- upset stomach (butterflies and nausea)

- increased perspiration and sweaty palms

- dizziness

- narrowing of the auditory range and tunnel vision

- erratic sleep patterns

Think back to a time when you were stressed about something. Did you experience these symptoms? Start paying attention to your physical reactions whenever you're faced with a challenge or threat. You may also notice the presence of one or more symptoms when you're generally feeling fine—if you do, check in with yourself to see if other symptoms are present. You may be more stressed than you think.

Control Your Attention

The greatest discovery of all time is that a person can change his
future by merely changing his attitude.
—OPRAH WINFREY, AMERICAN MEDIA MOGUL
AND ACTRESS (1954–)

Attention control is the SEAL version of positive self-talk. At the simplest level, it means to shift our attention from the negative by talking to ourselves positively. This is an active application of the DIRECT process for exercising control of your mind, which you learned under Principle 2, but in this case, we're using it to focus our attention in a crisis or challenging situation.

The nature of the outer, conscious mind is to receive input, process it through our story filter, and then make meaning out of it. A problem arises when too much of what flows through our minds is negative: The conscious mind dwells on negative things and obsesses about them. Sound familiar? It's well known that whatever we focus on tends to become our reality, even if the focus is on not wanting something. Negative input can plant seeds of destruction in our subconscious mind, which then partners with our conscious mind in a conspiracy for failure.

The art of positive self-talk is simply paying attention to your inner dialogue and directing it toward positive, performance-based language. Most people don't take the time to sit back and witness their own thoughts, which is an essential step toward realizing that our thoughts are not who we are. They don't control us. They're just thoughts. The only power they have is what we give them—what we feed them. Once you create that mental distance between you and your thoughts, you can start to tame and manage them. The DIRECT process will help you accomplish these tasks, but it can be a little clunky in the clutch. So I use another favorite tool when I need to shift my attention quickly.

The Native American legend "The Wolves Within" tells of an evil wolf and a good wolf that live inside us, constantly battling for control. Other versions describe the two opposing forces as Fear Dog and Courage Dog, which is what we use at SEALFIT. The lesson is that whichever dog you feed will win the fight. We can't kill Fear Dog because he's a part of us—remember, fear is natural and sometimes even useful—but we can weaken his power. Negative thoughts and energy feed Fear Dog, weakening us, leading to performance degradation and poor health. We can lock Fear Dog up and redirect his energy into assertiveness and discipline. Meanwhile, we need to feed Courage Dog. Positive thoughts and energy feed Courage Dog, strengthening the mind, body, and spirit. Feeding Courage Dog makes us more kind, patient, tolerant, powerful, and present. We'll avoid conflict and become better leaders. We won't hesitate to lean into the hard tasks; fear won't control us.

All you have to do is start asking yourself, "What dog am I feeding?" By paying attention to which dog you're feeding moment to moment, you'll begin to notice another level of your thought patterns. Again, as we discussed with regard to the DIRECT process, once you're aware of your patterns, you can better maintain a positive internal dialogue, which will manage your attention and keep it where it should be: on success. At the end of this chapter, you'll find an exercise and tips to help you. If you're on a team (and I don't know a single person who isn't part of some team in the broader context of the word), you can adapt the exercise so you serve as the "morale officer" of your group.

Simply explain the dogs of fear and courage to your teammates and, next time things start going south, interrupt any arguments or can't-do attitudes by saying: "Folks, what dog are we feeding right now? Let's feed the courage dog!" Bring awareness to the moment and help reframe arguments or problems toward the positive. Soon your team's attitude will shift for the better thanks to this new, very powerful tool.

Develop Emotional Resilience

An optimist is one who sees opportunity in every difficulty.
A pessimist is one who sees difficulty in every opportunity.
—L.P. JACKS, AMERICAN EDUCATOR AND PHILOSOPHER
(1860–1955)

In 1994, while at SEAL Team THREE, I had the opportunity to study an American hand-to-hand combat method called the Special Combat Aggressive Reactionary System (SCARS) with its founder, Jerry Peterson. As the intense 300-hour course progressed, I slowly realized my exhaustion went deeper than my strained muscles. It wasn't just the arduous physical training wearing me down—it was also the emotional roller coaster of getting my butt handed to me a couple hundred times a day. In the first few days, I felt awkward and tentative, and my SEAL classmates weren't much better. In fact, my biggest fear came from partnering with some of my classmates, loose cannons who were out of control and could easily break a bone or worse. I recall getting pissed at a fellow student as he flailed at me, knocking out my front tooth. My anger welled up and I took it to him the rest of the day. But that behavior earned me a rebuke from Jerry, who told me that a warrior who can't control and positively channel his emotions will lose every time. When your emotions are distracting you from focusing on your next target, you're naturally on the defensive . . . and in any situation where the other fighter is aggressive, you're toast.

Emotional resilience is instrumental to your ability to forge mental toughness—it's the power to bounce back quickly when circumstances conspire against you. How do you respond when you lose a job, are rejected, or get kicked in the groin? Do you allow negative emotions to take hold and cause an adverse or defensive reaction, undermining your arousal and attention control? Or do you remain the captain of your destiny, maintaining emotional control and coming back with a positive, offensive response that fuels your self-esteem and propels you forward?

Harness Your Emotions

You have heard that there are two types of people in the world—those whose glass is half-empty and those whose glass is half-full. In this broad-brush generalization, what we're really saying is that someone is completely negative or completely positive. The half-empty folks combine negative thinking with negative emotional states, locking themselves into a scarce worldview supported by feelings of scarcity. It's the opposite for the half-full folks. However, it's possible, as you learn the art of positivity, to be stuck in emotional purgatory where you think positively but feel negatively. Many of you may have read about or even practiced positive self-talk. But that is only part of the equation. One must speak, visualize, and feel positively in order to be aligned in positivity. Otherwise, the emotional states counteract the positive self-talk and imagery, leading to weak results. The starting point is emotional awareness: Are you emotionally positive or negative?

I realized during the SCARS course that I was mentally positive but emotionally negative. When my classmate knocked my tooth out, I remained positive mentally, saying the right things in my head about the situation, such as "no big deal, easy day, could have been worse," but resentment that I now had to deal with a medical issue as the result of my partner's carelessness wormed its way beneath and in between those thoughts. Because the intense training required 100 percent of my focus, my personal pity party slowed me down, and the resentment and anger caused my muscles to tighten, which was counterproductive to my controlled combat moves. Once I became aware of my negative emotions, I used an early version of the DIRECT process to override them with positive ones. For the remainder of the course, I worked on stopping negative feelings in their tracks and replaced or recharacterized them—feelings of anger became determination, and I replaced feelings of uncertainty with excitement about

WAY OF THE SEAL DRILL

. . . .

Transform Your Emotions

DIRECT works in a slightly different way when it comes to emotional control. To gain control of your feelings and transmute negative emotions into healthier expressions, you must approach the process with an attitude of acceptance—when you first detect the emotion, allow it to exist in your body. Bring your awareness to where it resides in your skin and muscles. Now, use deep breathing to get some space between you and the emotion, perhaps combined with a mantra like "I am not my thoughts and feelings." This distance will allow you to interdict and then release the emotion so you can redirect your focus and energy into a healthier expression. Communicate your new state to your subconscious through positive self-talk and simple visualization, seeing yourself in the positive emotional state you wish to achieve.

To practice doing this, see the list on the next page of primary negative emotions and their healthier counterparts. In a quiet place, sit and relax, and then close your eyes. Try conjuring these negative, primary emotions one at a time—perhaps you can recall

learning something new. I sought to stop myself every time I noticed my emotions turning negative or counterproductive. Immediately I started to gain confidence, and became more effective.

You're already using the DIRECT process (Detect, Interdict, Redirect, Energize, Communicate, Train) to control your mind and your attention. Now, start extending this practice to your emotions. After all, besides the root emotions of love and fear (emotions we experience in the very first moments of our lives, forever characterizing the positive and negative realities of our human experience), most emoa time when you felt anger, for example. Recall the thoughts running through your head and how you felt physically. Notice how your body, even in this exercise, begins to reproduce those same feelings. Now, DIRECT the negative emotion into a more positive expression and note how you feel physically with each shift. If it helps, conjure the memory of a time you actually felt or expressed these positive qualities to make the experience more tangible.

Primary Emotion	Healthy Expression
Anger	Clarity, determination
Fear	Alertness, eagerness
Greed	Contentment, generosity
Doubt	Curiosity, excitement
Jealousy	Acceptance, love

Training with this drill will help familiarize you with this process so that the next time you find yourself experiencing a negative emotion in response to an event, you'll automatically turn to the DIRECT process and transform your emotional landscape, bouncing back into the fray with renewed vigor.

tions are stored thought energy. You can witness negative emotions, interdict them, and then redirect them into positive emotions. The trick is to learn to recognize how emotions feel rather than how they make us think. We experience emotions in our bodies as well as our minds—that's why we often feel the physical reaction even though we may suppress or deny an emotion mentally. When you're angry, for instance, your muscles may tighten, or you may hold your breath when you're afraid. Just as tightening certain muscles, limiting breathing, and holding certain thoughts and images in your mind can limit the experience of an emotion, the opposite is true. You can learn to relax those same muscles, expand your breathing, and change your mind, you can allow yourself to more fully feel something or feel it for the first time consciously.

Build Your Self-Esteem

Negative emotions are debilitating, minimizing your sense of self. Belief in your inherent goodness is critical for self-esteem to flourish. When you train your new, positive emotional states using the "T" step of the DIRECT method until they become part of your makeup, you will naturally elevate your self-esteem. Consistent application of positive self-talk as you manage your attention will multiply positive feelings about yourself as well. A regular gratitude practice through journaling can help you stay focused on the positive and is especially helpful when negative thoughts and feelings threaten to overwhelm you. As part of your morning ritual, try listing in your journal at least one good thing about yourself. During your evening ritual, list at least one thing for which you are grateful. (The outlines for these rituals appear in Appendix 2.) Don't stop at one if you feel moved to list more! If you're feeling particularly awful and nothing positive about yourself or your day immediately springs to mind, you can always write down something like "My desire to be better is one good thing I recognize about myself," and "Today I am just grateful that I'm alive, healthy, and employed."

Cultivate Optimism

Remain full of faith and optimism that things will work out, that they happen for a purpose. This aspect of emotional resilience overlaps with our spiritual development. As you work in the Way of the SEAL, you will find yourself developing a strong will to succeed, an undercurrent of optimism bolstered by each win you achieve. Much as meeting your 20X challenges and practicing other mental toughness techniques increase your confidence, the overall experience of watching your self-imposed limitations dissolve as you meet each target and accomplish each mission will strengthen your warrior spirit. Note that I speak of spirit somewhat removed from religion, but if you are a religious person, your beliefs can definitely become yet another source of fuel for positive spiritual growth. Some of my students have even reported that their relationship to their faith tradition grew deeper as their own sense of spirit expanded.

Regardless of how you define your spirituality or the source of your spirit, you must direct its power toward cultivating an optimistic outlook. Don't be a victim of life's challenges; rather, be a warrior on an endless journey seeking the most valuable lessons life can offer. The exercise "Finding the Silver Lining" on page 132 will prove useful for this practice.

Take Your Eyes Off Yourself

Those who are self-absorbed tend to be defensive and less emotionally mature than those who serve others. SEALs learn to take their eyes off themselves and put them on their teammates to win. Over time, this effort becomes part of them and the bond of brotherhood is formed. As you do this yourself, you will gain humility and a generous attitude, strengthening your emotional resolve. This is an important developmental stage for all of us, so it deserves careful consideration.

Authentic teammates are attentive to each other's needs and work with an attitude of cooperation and service, pitching in when needed. They don't ignore the team's common needs, such as cleaning the sink and emptying the trash, either. Ask yourself, "How can I make the leader's job easier? How can I make my teammates more effective?" Everyone steps up to play at an entirely different level with a service attitude. Note, however, that service provided grudgingly or as part of a task list is not service, but an obligation. Where service carries a powerful positive force multiplier, depositing energy into an individual or team's spiritual bank account and uplifting both the recipient and the giver, fulfilling an obligation is neutral or can even be negative, withdrawing from the account.

Set Effective Goals

Don't believe the world owes you a living;
the world owes you nothing—it was here first.
—ROBERT JONES BURDETTE, AMERICAN CLERIC AND HUMORIST
(1844–1914)

With Principle 3, you learned how to rank your targets for highest value so you won't get distracted from your priorities, which in turn helps you remain front-sight focused on achieving mission success. Now let's take a step back to look at how you're choosing your targets, and your overall mission, in the first place.

Each time you set a goal—whether it is big or long-term as in your overall mission or small and shorter-term as in the missions to hit your targets along the way to your primary objective—you ignite a spiral of success that feeds your mental toughness. You're giving yourself something to strive for (a "why"), something to visualize and focus on for positive momentum. And each time you achieve your goal, the thrill of success and the surge of confidence you receive expand your sense of self, enhance your emotional resilience, and make it that much easier to tackle the next mission. But you're much more likely to achieve your goals if they are set properly in the first place.

Well-stated goals are precise, positive, and written down. They are also measurable and have an associated, and appropriate, time-frame: Too short and either they aren't meaty enough goals, or you're setting yourself up for failure; too long and your goals fall off the radar for lack of urgency. Your goals must be achievable in that you have the potential to accomplish them with the skills and resources available to you. Which leads to the last element of proper goal setting: Your goals must be realistic for you and your life situation. These attributes form the acronym SMART—Specific, Measurable, Achievable, Realistic, and Timely or Time-Bound.

All your goals—whether at the interim target or overall mission level—should be SMART goals. Then you will further zero in on the highest-value targets out of several options (or rank your targets in order of priority) using the FITS tool we learned with Principle 3.

The tougher things get, the smaller your goals should become. These "microgoals" should be laser-focused on achievement of a target or a refined subset of your overall mission—this is benchmarking at work. While my trainees' arms are shaking, I don't encourage them to focus on holding their push-up position for forty-five minutes but for just one minute. During Hell Week, I didn't focus on getting my Trident but on finishing the current physical training round safely with my team intact.

Avoid creating too many goals at one time, which can defuse your front-sight focus. Remember, SEALs focus on one mission at a time—both at the macro, or overall mission, level and at the micro, or target, level. An unrealistic time frame can also lead to frustration. Unwillingness to modify your goals to meet reality (remember that no plan survives contact with the enemy) can indicate inflexible thinking, the opposite of the innovation we're trying to cultivate. If you lack process goals or a "being" purpose, you can become absorbed in achievement without enough focus on actual, lasting improvement (but understand that it's often necessary to include achievement goals on the way to a bigger "being" purpose). Finally, I can't emphasize enough how important it is to check with yourself daily, measuring and probing your progress. This ensures you stay on track, maintain momentum, and hold yourself accountable! The Exercises section at the end of this chapter will walk you through the WOS goal-setting process in more detail.

Visualize Powerfully

Nurture your mind with great thoughts,
for you will never go any higher than you think.
—BENJAMIN DISRAELI, BRITISH PRIME MINISTER
AND PARLIAMENTARIAN (1804–1881)

What if, during a challenging situation, you are focused on solid short-term goals, steeped in positive self-talk, and performing deep breathing, but your internal imagery is about disaster? Guess what: You will fail. That is why visualization shows up again as a mental toughness tool. Visualization is practiced in three primary forms: guided meditation, mental projection, and mental rehearsal. Guided meditation describes the use of a scripted series of images that facilitate a particular experience for your mind, typically to promote relaxation or healing or to tap into your subconscious. This versatile type of visualization, which includes practices such as the Still Water Runs Deep or the mind gym, is used in many spiritual traditions and schools of self-improvement, as it has myriad practical applications. But, to forge mental toughness, mental projection and mental rehearsal are better suited.

As we learned in Principle 1 with the "Future Me" visualization, in a mental projection, you visualize yourself achieving your goal. For maximum results, imagine the scene as vividly as possible—notice the colors, hear the sounds, smell the scents, taste the flavors, and feel the emotions as if you were actually there. Then reinforce this vision through repetition or internal "visits." This plants a potent seed in your subconscious that can transform the possible future into a probable future; you're activating your subconscious mind to work in harmony with your conscious mind.

In Principle 3, we discussed virtual dirt diving, a mental rehearsal in which you practice a skill or rehearse an action in your mind. This leads to an alignment of the inner and outer as your mental rehearsals, over time, imprint the practiced skill in your subconscious mind and nervous system. Research has shown that dedication to mental rehearsals will produce results similar to those of live rehearsals, with improved performance flowing from the familiarity you've built. Tiger Woods credits his superior success on the circuit to mental rehearsals, coupled with swinging the club more than any other golfer.

Both mental projection and mental rehearsal are important for mental toughness because staying the course through tough situations requires us to manage our fears. By "experiencing" something you fear through visualization, you can mitigate the fear response when you face it "live." For example, if you're afraid of public speaking, mentally rehearse giving a speech and project an image of yourself speaking confidently and capturing the attention of an adoring audience. This can make the actual experience less daunting.

So much of our performance hinges on our ability to master our minds. My trainees get very excited when visualization clicks with them; it's truly a game changer.

★ ★ ★ EXERCISES ★ ★ ★

BOX BREATHING

Position yourself in a seated meditation or other comfortable position. Your back should be straight, your chin slightly tucked, gaze soft or eyes closed. Place your hands lightly on your knees and bring your attention to your breath.

- Take a few deep diaphragm breaths slowly, with a four-count inhale followed immediately by a four-count complete exhalation. Repeat this for four rounds as a warm-up.

- Now, begin your Box Breathing practice by taking a four-count breath slowly through your nose.

- Hold your breath for a count of four. Concentrate on the quality of the breath and noticing what enters your mind. If your mind wanders, gently bring it back to the breath.

- Exhale slowly through the nose to a count of four.

- Hold your breath again for a count of four. Pay attention to the quality of the hold and watch your mind.

Repeat this process for a minimum of five minutes and practice it until you can do it for up to twenty minutes at a time. Over time, you can also increase the duration of the inhale, exhale, and hold period. Seek to settle your thoughts and any fidgeting. If a thought arises, just let it go and bring your attention back to the breathing. Use Box Breathing as part of your morning ritual (see Appendix 2) and during the day as "spot training" whenever you have the opportunity—such as when reading e-mail—or when you feel excess stress building up.

TURNING STRESS INTO SUCCESS

To control your response to stress—whether chronic, low-grade stress such as financial worries or acute, extreme stress such as with combat—you must practice and master a three-stage process. This incorporates the DIRECT process for mental control and emotional resilience (Detect, Interdict, Redirect, Energize, Communicate, and Train) from Principle 2's Exercises and takes it to the next level by merging it with deep breathing to control your physiological reactions.

Stage 1: As you learned to do with negative thoughts and emotions, practice the DIRECT process to perceive and interdict automatic responses to stressful events as they arise and begin expressing themselves through your mind and body.

Stage 2: Take control and reverse the sympathetic nervous system response with Box Breathing. This will prevent the retriggering of the stress response.

Stage 3: Maintain calm and focus under pressure by continuing to breathe deeply minus the box structure (no need to count or hold your breath in between inhales and exhales) while adding positive self-talk and even a quick mental projection that reinforces your self-esteem or cultivates optimism. The deep, controlled breathing process coupled with positive attention control and imagery will enable you to override any destructive thoughts or emotions sneaking in. Don't forget to monitor your responses and the language you're using to keep everything positive and healthy as per our earlier drill.

As you practice, you'll find stress dissipating in the face of improved clarity, focus, and resilience. As you recognize these developments in yourself, you'll naturally feel more confident, which continues to feed your upward spiral of success.

WHAT DOG ARE YOU FEEDING?

Start building awareness of your mental state by forcing periodic mental breaks throughout your day. Stop whatever you're doing and quietly examine your thoughts and "feeling state" in the moment. If necessary, identify your feelings by labeling them with words such as anger, jealousy, peacefulness, excitement, and so on. If it isn't immediately obvious, you'll know whether you are stressed and feeling negative or in the flow and feeling positive once you recognize which dog your words belong to: Courage Dog or Fear Dog. Once you've identified your mental and emotional state, again you will use the DIRECT process to maintain a positive mind and emotional state.

Tip 1: Place a rubber band around your wrist. Whenever you notice the rubber band, snap it and bring your attention to your thoughts and feelings at that exact moment. This is particularly useful if you're always on the go. You can substitute anything for the rubber band that will stand out to you as atypical and get your attention.

Tip 2: Set a timer (using your phone, perhaps) for every two or three hours during the day. When the timer goes off, follow the same steps as above. This is great for an office or home setting.

Tip 3: Whichever method you use, practice daily for a week, and journal your thoughts and results. When you feel yourself recognizing and DIRECTing your state of mind as it unfolds, reduce practice to three times per week, until you feel it has become a habit to recognize which dog you're feeding moment to moment.

SETTING SMART GOALS

With a journal, sit quietly and contemplate your passions, values, and purpose as you defined them with Principle 1. Now consider all the things you would like to be, do, or have in your life. What about in the next year? The next five years? List them all.

- Select the three life goals or missions that most excite
  you and will move you toward fulfilling your purpose,
  then break these down further into three-year goals and
  one-year goals that will move you toward your primary
  objectives. Write these goals (read: targets) out in SMART
  terms: Specific, Measurable, Achievable, Realistic, and
  Timely or Time-Bound. Describe what it would be like to
  accomplish these goals and what it would be like if you do
  not accomplish them.

- Take a few deep breaths and get comfortable. Enter your mind gym and, using the projection screen you set up there, see yourself accomplishing these goals in as much detail as you possibly can, as if you were actually living these future moments right now, or as if they've already happened.

- Repeat this process for your top three quarterly or three-month micro-goals, which should be tied to your selected one-year goals.

When you're finished, clean up your list so you have a clear and uncluttered reference and use the Focus Plan worksheets in Appendix 1 to organize everything and to further break your quarterly goals down into monthly, weekly, and daily goals. Commit to reviewing your Focus Plans daily as part of your morning ritual, as outlined in Appendix 2.

You may already be in the process of pursuing some of these goals using the tools we've learned so far in *The Way of the SEAL*. That's great—keep it up! But make sure you subject any pre-existing goals to this process to ensure you are truly focused on the right goals so you can guarantee a mental toughness win.

BREAK THINGS

The moment you say "I know everything" is the end of your growth.
—SHARON LEE, AMERICAN AUTHOR (1952–)

"We have a problem, Mark." My CFO, Lisa, walked into my office with a worried look. We had just launched a new website and store for my e-commerce business, NavySEALs.com. The third-party platform powering the new site, which maximized evolving web technology, was an attempt to gain back some ground after we lost 40 percent of our merchandising business practically overnight during the 2008 economic downturn. Unfortunately, it looked like things weren't going as planned. "The migration failed, and our organic search is down 80 percent," Lisa told me.

She couldn't have delivered worse news. In just a few months, we had gone from a thriving online store grossing $125,000 per month to about $2,000 a month. We were out of any meaningful capital and now we'd lost years of momentum in one fell swoop because our new web developers had screwed up. Organic search can't be forced; it takes time for website traffic to grow. I could keep the business marginally alive, but I knew it would no longer support me, let alone a staff. I decided I needed to break things.

I retreated to my office and turned to my mental tools to contemplate and envision what the future of my business could look like. I had invested heavily in NavySEALs.com after turning my back on government contracting in 2007. My intent was to maintain NavySEALs.com as a cash-flow machine while I developed the SEALFIT concept, starting with a small training center. In the past, I would have pulled out all stops to recover the business, probably hiring someone to fix the website while attempting to scrounge up more funds. In such a situation, I would normally recommend to an entrepreneur to find another way to make it work. And it's common to feel like, "I've already put so much into this, I can't just let it go."

Now, however, as I looked at the bigger picture, I realized it would take too much time and too much money, and I just didn't feel enough passion for it. I made a conscious effort to break the mold of my "I can do this no matter what" thinking and let the old business go so I could focus on the new. As I did so, I started to feel energy shifting inside me and a growing optimism. I recognized that an opportunity had emerged out of the chaos, and I had a sense of "knowing" this was the right path, something I hadn't felt strongly since leaving the SEALs and then government contracting.

I needed to streamline quickly in order to keep what I had afloat, so by the end of that day, I had decided to lay off the small NavySEALs.com team and reorient my expectations for the business. It wasn't an easy decision, but checking in with my stand and my gut reinforced for me that my unhappiness and deep discomfort (who wants to lay people off?) was of the temporary kind related to making tough but necessary decisions. I felt confident that it was the right move. Fortunately, I had kept the team in the loop during the crisis, so they weren't blindsided. Though losing a job and having to let people go are both standard in business, I believe the latter should always be done with grace.

The next morning my wife, Sandy, and I poked through the few orders, trying to make sense of details we hadn't been involved in for years. Sandy helped me tremendously during that trying time as I built SEALFIT brick by brick. With her help and that of her daughter

Cindy and Cindy's husband, Rich, we also recovered NavySEALs.com and turned it into a sustainable business again. It took two years before I earned another paycheck, but as SEALFIT took flight out of the rubble of NavySEALs.com, I learned that you often need to break things before you can remake them into something better. This is achieved through:

- applying total commitment
- failing forward fast
- navigating gaps for opportunity
- innovating and adapting quickly

In this chapter, I'll teach you to harness the power of these tenets for yourself.

Apply Total Commitment

Do or do not; there is no try.
—YODA IN *THE EMPIRE STRIKES BACK*

In 2004, security of elected leaders in Iraq was a major problem, and in the lexicon of "nation building," it was a State Department job. State waived off on it, though, because they just couldn't operate in the chaos and extremely high threat level of the combat zone. Instead, they handed the mission off to SEAL Team ONE under Commander W.

The commander and his team needed to break things quickly for this effort to succeed: It was one thing to marshal a VIP out of a danger zone, but it was another altogether to protect five elected officials of a foreign government 24/7 in the most dangerous place on earth. So how do you turn a static security detail designed to protect one person, one time, at one location into an aggressive, persistent mission dealing with multiple people and daily activities and threats? Well, ST-1 figured it out and had the mission up and running in sixty days. The concepts they employed to rapidly shift fire and learn the new skills form the basis of this chapter.

Burn Your Boat

True commitment, the type your teammates can rely on as if their lives depended on it, requires you to burn your boat upon the shore of action. You must then press forward because you have removed the way out, igniting the fire of challenge. Commander W. and his team demonstrated that there is no "maybe" when you make an important decision. Asking the SEALs to do security detail is like asking the Terminator to babysit, and yet when the call came down, the answer was "Yes, sir, we've got this!"

Certainty is a powerful energetic force essential for breaking inertia and developing momentum. The seed of certainty is found in commitment, a one-way street. You can't partly commit or potentially commit. When you deliver a powerful "Yes, I've got this!" you inject a positive intent and energy into a project that is palpable. Conversely, "I'll give it a try" is a dull thud of defeatism. This is partly attitude and partly action. When NavySEALs.com failed, for example, I could have called it a day. Instead, I committed to reinventing my business, reorganizing my priorities, and adjusting my expectations.

Have you noticed how the value our society places on commitment has slid? We've crept from insisting that "you do what you say, period," to honoring "I tried and gave it my best" to accepting "I meant to get to it, but something else came up." Take a cue from Yoda, who forcefully mentors Luke: "Do or do not; there is no try!" You must commit with everything you have; otherwise say "no" or "not now."

Find a Way or Make One

For elite operators, commitment doesn't mean you already know how you're going to get it done. "Find a way or make a way" was our motto in the SEALs. It means you will commit and then figure it out. Since no challenge is completely new or unique, to break the mold of current thinking, you'll want to meld ideas from the past with informed predictions about the future to come up with new solutions for the present.

In 2004, many people felt things were improving in Iraq. After the White House tasked the SEALs with the security detail, Commander W. did a ground-level assessment and realized things would actually get worse as insurgents stepped up efforts to dismantle the fledgling democracy and knock the knees out of our mission there. But he didn't work in a vacuum to figure out how to secure the Iraqi leaders from imminent death. He and ST-1 first looked at the existing State Department protocols. They reached out to SEALs who'd protected President Karzai in Afghanistan. They liaised with private contractors like Blackwater and Triple Canopy, who had been protecting convoys in Iraq. They explored new technologies they could use to detect and track threats and brainstormed ideas for how to organize and work with their Iraqi counterparts. They gathered, filtered, and sifted the golden nuggets into the pan of their mission plan. Finally, they molded these nuggets into completely new standard operating procedures (SOPs) and strategies for a mission never before accomplished on this scale and in the heart of a combat zone. In the beginning, they had only their willingness to break things and their commitment to finding a way to remake them better. In the end they avoided, prevented, or defended against over four hundred attempts of varying types on the leaders' lives and trained an Iraqi force to replace them, all while continuing to conduct direct action missions, a remarkable feat for a team of just over one hundred operators.

SEAL Team ONE "broke" the typical defensive protocol of a protection detail, which was designed to protect one individual or family in an environment where threats exist but aren't always active, and created a new approach that would function more effectively in what was essentially a frontline combat situation with multiple parties coming at the new electorate from multiple angles. Instead of just providing a protective shield and then defending when attacked, ST-1 went further to identify potential threats to the Iraqi leaders. Then they had their direct action team track these enemies, fix their location, and head them off before they could launch an assault. This blended several distinct mission sets into one hybrid operation.

For instance, when SEAL intelligence identified a threat from a high-level Al Qaeda operative to then President Maliki, the SEALs immediately began monitoring the suspect's communications via cell phone, video, and blogs as well as his contacts with other known insurgents. The team connected dots from informants culled from the local population and who proved trustworthy. The information all pointed to an attack in the planning stages, destined for the middle of Baghdad. Using their newly developed SOPs for finding bad guys, the intel team was finally able to "fix" the target at a known location and at a known time. Commander W. and his SEALs mounted a direct-action mission to capture the insurgent before he could carry out his attack.

This operation and others of this nature were difficult to pull off but crucial to keeping the bad guys on the defensive. The SEALs didn't wait for the threat to come to them—they aggressively moved toward the threat. Anyone planning to hit the protected Iraqi leaders soon learned there was a new sheriff in town. There's no way of knowing exactly how many would-be terrorists backed off in the wake of this effort, but it undoubtedly caused many to pause and shift course to find easier targets.

Fail Forward Fast

Success consists of going from failure to failure
without loss of enthusiasm.
—WINSTON CHURCHILL, BRITISH PRIME MINISTER (1874–1965)

I believe the world is chaotic and destiny favors the prepared. Unfortunately, sometimes chaos just refuses the harness, no matter how well you bulletproof your mission and how committed you are to finding a way. Moving forward despite chaotic conditions—and sometimes because of them—is inherently risky, and since we don't shy from risk in the Way of the SEAL, you will inevitably experience failure, probably more often than you succeed, actually.

The good news is that, culturally, failure is not as shameful as it once might have been—it's become almost commonplace for an individual to lose his job, to see her business go belly-up, or to file for bankruptcy (either in business or personally). In today's fast-paced world, new technologies change industries overnight. With the business, social, and political landscapes shifting like quicksand, "failing forward fast" is more important now than ever. When you deliberately break something, you must shift your perspective so that you both expect and welcome failure—you will seek it out because that is where the opportunities for personal and professional growth lie hidden. In fact, you're getting it out of the way, knowing that only failure will bring the insights and lessons necessary to remake things better.

During one of my early programs, we had a steelworker from Pittsburgh who walked into the ocean for a swimming exercise and sank right to the bottom. He couldn't swim and didn't float, but he was too scared to tell me so he just went in and down! We got him out after a moment of panic. It had made sense to incorporate ocean swimming into the program, based as it was on SEAL training. However, as more nonmilitary professionals sought to train with us, we suspected we would inevitably attract people who couldn't swim at that level. Instead of knee-jerk reacting to this obvious failure (read: learning opportunity) and scratching the water work, we rethought the process. We couldn't take all participants swimming in deep water because of the risk, but we could put them in waist-deep and have them carry logs or go through "surf torture" (sitting at water's edge with their arms interlocked). This removed the actual risk of drowning while maintaining the perceived risk and challenge of the cold and the forceful water.

Alden Mills, a SEAL teammate of mine, demonstrated the power of failing forward fast in a big way when he launched his hugely successful Perfect Pushup product. I recall playing with his first product, the Body Rev, as we evaluated it to sell at NavySEALs.com. I couldn't figure out how to use the darn thing. The Body Rev used a gyroscopic motion in a device you held in your hands and rotated in a circle in front of your body (hence the name Body Rev) to develop core and upper-body strength. Alden had raised $1.5 million around the concept and produced an infomercial aimed at the women's fitness market. Apparently, I wasn't the only one who couldn't figure it out. The product failed, largely because consumers found it too complicated to use, and because Alden had targeted too small a corner of the fitness market. Alden burned through all but $25,000 of his money with little to show for it.

This is where his SEAL-taught ability to embrace failure as a teacher came in handy. His timeline was so short, his pockets so shallow, and the naysayers so loud that he put his blinders and earmuffs on and focused on this one problem with such a controlled intensity that he was able to solve it with a home-run hit in a few short months. Rather than tweaking the failed product for a different market, which might have been a safer, easier half-step, or closing his business entirely and moving on, he decided to invent another, simpler product—the Perfect Pushup. The product took stationary push-up handles and put them on a rotating bevel, allowing the user's wrists, elbows, and shoulders to rotate during the push-up for a more ergonomically functional movement. Learning from his mistakes, he relied this time on print ads in a few men's sports magazines (a market he knew more about, which was also a more proven market for such products than the women's magazines he'd previously targeted), using his own credit cards to buy the ad space rather than borrowing money for a bigger campaign. He was soon profitable enough to self-fund an infomercial, which garnered the Perfect Pushup nationwide awareness and placement in over 24,000 retail stores in just one year.

Systematize Trial and Error

Failing forward fast is embedded in the culture and rules of the SEALs. Good leaders see the important role failure plays and embrace it. You can't be squeamish about blowback. When things don't go well, which will happen occasionally, there can be no witch hunt if good intentions were involved. Instead, seek to learn what didn't work and why, pick up the pieces, and move forward with a new approach. If you aren't in a position to change the culture of your organization, start at a grassroots level by encouraging your team to take more risks, and then provide top cover for them by taking the hit if they fail. This may sound risky for your own career, and it could be, but it will lead to more momentum for your team and more growth for you as a leader. Keep your focus on the big picture: Your growth and success are what's important, and your evolution into an elite leader may not necessarily include hanging on to your current job! If your boss doesn't agree and invites you to leave, then you can rest assured that another business leader, one who embraces this philosophy, would love to know about your initiative. As you show a willingness to be vulnerable, you can inspire those higher up in the organization to do the same, or at least to improve their risk tolerance as they see the results you're getting.

What I am suggesting is that you systematize trial and error for yourself, your team, and ideally your organization. Failing forward fast allows everyone to learn and gain momentum together in a rapid process. Failure is simply a step in a learning process that looks like this:

1. Try something new.

2. Fail.

3. Analyze (a) the lessons we learned, and (b) how we can modify our approach to gain momentum and prevent the failure again.

4. Implement changes for the next iteration.

5. Incorporate the insights personally and at the team level to shift your thinking for another go-round, and perhaps adjust the system or process itself to reflect the new knowledge.

6. Try it again and repeat steps 2 through 5 until you've succeeded in your mission.

This process conditions you to fail forward fast. Failure becomes an expected event, not a disruptive "all-stop" moment where we slay the instigator. Failing forward fast must become a positive imperative that develops momentum to overcome inevitable challenges, moving you constantly toward new solutions. Team members are happier and perform better because their intrinsic quest for growth is met. No one is stifled or punished for taking risks on behalf of the organization.

Eliminating Risk Aversion

Often a fear of failure or an aversion to risk because of that fear contributes to failure itself. Holding back at the moment of execution in a dive could cause you to hit the board and crack your skull open. Not taking decisive action on a business deal or stock pick because you are fearful of taking a loss will lead to missed opportunities and a failure to learn and grow—and it could even have more dire consequences, like your business going bankrupt. Risk-averse souls see failure as a validation that:

- they were not right for the job
- the team messed things up
- the market/universe turned against them
- the project or business was always doomed to failure

Though all may be true at some level, these weak beliefs are not very helpful, nor will they propel you forward toward results. Taking responsibility and learning from your mistakes, rather than looking to place blame, is the Way of the SEAL. The thing failed . . . so what? Next! It would have been fruitless for me to blame and attack my web developer for the NavySEALs.com debacle. Failure does not deserve to be addressed with recrimination or pity. Rather, failure must be honored for the insight it provides. Failure is the grist for learning; it is our teacher. Without taking risk, we can't fail, and so we don't learn or grow toward elite performance and top-shelf solutions.

Navigate Gaps for Opportunity

If you're looking for a big opportunity, seek out a big problem.

—H. JACKSON BROWN, BESTSELLING AUTHOR OF *LIFE'S LITTLE INSTRUCTION BOOK* (1940–)

Life will bring you plenty of opportunity in the form of failure and, as you embrace the concept of failing forward fast with intention, you will accelerate toward opportunities for learning and growth. But as a WOS leader, you can and should also proactively seek out opportunities for breaking things so you can remake them better.

The speed of technological advancement has accelerated change in all areas of commerce, government, and our personal lives. As these new realities depart from the old boundary lines, gaps open, and in these gaps arise numerous opportunities. During transition periods such as we are currently experiencing, there will be more chaos, more reality gaps, and more opportunities. These opportunities are yours to grab.

Operate in the Present

Most people won't even spot these opportunities because they are always looking over their shoulders, obsessing about how things used to be, wishing for a return to the old days. These people tend to be pessimistic and unsatisfied because they're pining for a return to something already gone. It slows them down as they deny change and aren't able or willing to see into the future.

A smaller segment of the population is always looking to the future and hoping things will change for the better while simultaneously fearing the worst. Statements such as "I can't wait until" or "When I get that new promotion" combined with negative "What if?" obsessing indicate this orientation. This type of person, though, can get stuck in the rut of hoping things will work out better next time instead of learning from past mistakes, which virtually guarantees he or she will continue perpetuating those mistakes. "Forward-time" thinkers also often miss opportunities because they lack the courage to take action. Much of our fear in today's relatively safe world stems from an imagined but unknown future, so those who orient their minds toward that future by visualizing failure and all the horrible things that might happen find themselves trapped in a constant loop of negative input. Unless and until you learn to visualize success and an abundant future, "forward-time" thinking condemns your brain to a negative bias. Powerful and courageous action is difficult, if not impossible, from a negative state.

The creative mind operates in the present, while the rational, thinking mind rests in the past or future. Therefore, you must be able to tap into all three without getting stuck. You want to be optimistic and goal-oriented for the future, and then learn from and reconcile history. Finally, you must remain front-sight focused on new opportunities in the present. If you can readily shift focus from future to past to present, you will easily be able to spot the gaps between old and new realities and detect openings for breaking things that others miss.

Refining your mind so you can readily shift focus from future to past to present is the first step. To use this principle effectively, you will also want to look for weaknesses in your competitors' thinking models. Combining this knowledge with an understanding of how their systems are structured and where they are breaking down will allow you to spot hidden opportunities. Sun Tzu said more than 2,000 years ago that if you know yourself but not your enemy, for every battle you win you will also lose one. However, if you know yourself and your enemy, in one hundred battles you will see victory every time.

That all sounds great, but Sun Tzu's theory assumes that your mind is able to recognize and process any bits of information it encounters. It's difficult to achieve this kind of multifaceted knowledge when you're handicapped, as most of us are, by mental blind spots.

Identify and Destroy Blind Spots

The mind takes in an enormous amount of information every moment and must filter that information before it can make sense of it. The mind settles into certain ritualistic patterns or ways of thinking that are familiar and comfortable. In teams or cultures, these patterns get burned into the system as they are repeated, formalized, and then trained. They blind those in the system to other patterns of thought or ways of doing things, which keeps opportunities hidden from view. The best leaders are always on the lookout to shatter these ritualized behaviors in order to avoid blind spots.

While at SEAL Team THREE, I was tasked with a mission to test the Navy Explosive Ordnance Disposal team's anti-swimmer dolphins. These dolphins are trained to bar enemy divers from infiltrating sensitive waterways. The routine drill was to just dive toward the target and let the dolphins try to find you. When they did, they popped you in the facemask, hard. I'm sure they loved the game, but we didn't like it much. Besides, we wanted to derive some real training value from this mission. My team of five swim pairs got in the water at midnight. As we hugged the bottom of the channel where the dolphins had trouble using their natural sonar, I turned on a small handheld sonar device I had snuck into my wet suit. To the dolphins, it must have sounded like a rock concert at the bottom of the sea. My swim buddy and I sailed through to the target, as did all but one of the swim pairs, who received a facemask-busting kiss from one of the confused mammals.

The point of this story is that the EOD team, like any team in a system that does things the same way repeatedly, was exposed to risk because of blind spots that prevented them from seeing new ways of operating. I came in and saw the routine drill wasn't being taken seriously by the EOD team—they were comfortable with the status quo and obviously didn't consider that enemy swimmers might use simple unconventional tactics against the dolphins. That type of thinking gets you killed in combat, and it leads to losing market share or worse in business. To achieve victory every time requires us to navigate opportunity gaps, and then innovate and adapt rapidly to fill the gaps before others notice them.

Innovate and Adapt Quickly

Every man with a new idea is a crank
until the idea succeeds.
—MARK TWAIN, AMERICAN AUTHOR AND HUMORIST
(1835–1910)

The motto of the Marine Corps is the very worthy "Semper Fidelis," which means "Always Faithful." Marines are always faithful to each other, to the Corps, and to America—God bless them for that. With a nod to these brothers and sisters, an unwritten motto of the SEALs is "Semper Gumby," meaning "Always Flexible." This motto, a reference to the rubber-toy comic hero who can bend and mold to fit any situation, suggests one reason why SEALs can operate in the most chaotic scenarios and quickly navigate opportunity gaps in the systems to dominate the battle space. It is not their overwhelming firepower or supersecret technologies. No, it is their very human skill of innovating and adapting on demand.

For example, during the first Iraq war, Desert Storm, my friend Lieutenant Dietz and his small platoon of SEALs faced a challenge during their mission: They needed to transfer a large number of C-4 explosives to shore without detection, but that would require either a large, easily spotted vessel or multiple dangerous trips for SEALs in order to swim in what they could carry. Then a junior enlisted SEAL suggested using boogie boards to float the C-4 sacks into the surf zone. Stunned, my buddy Dietz immediately saw the brilliance of this unconventional idea. Certainly no one had considered using boogie boards in a special operations mission before, but the solution addressed all their needs. The call back to HQ for the boards raised some eyebrows, but the mission's success validated the concept.

This kind of flexibility is key to the SEALs' ability to take advantage of opportunities hidden to others. Their ability to act decisively on those opportunities gives them the momentum for victory.

Break Inertia with Decisive Action

After many years of SEAL training, martial arts, and yoga, I noticed how these traditions mirrored one another in many ways as warrior development models. I wanted to fuse their best practices into one integral training model. When my short foray into government contracting ended in 2007, my opportunity for this new pursuit arrived, yet I had no clear idea what business model might work to deliver such a training model to the public. Rather than study from afar, researching it from every angle, I decided to get my hands dirty and learn "on the fly." So I decisively threw myself into the challenge by opening a CrossFit gym (a functional fitness training system from which the SEALs had adopted some aspects) with the dual intent of furthering my own skills and knowledge and figuring out the right business model by trying different tactics. I started leading a class called SEALFIT and developed the Kokoro Camp to test my theories, teaching an early version of my integral training approach, which included CrossFit, strength and endurance development, mental toughness skills, and yoga. I also began studying all I could about mental toughness and performance psychology so I could back up my experiential learning with the proper vocabulary and research. I knew that I needed to become a subject-matter expert if I wanted to sustain my new career as a trainer of character. I could not afford to avoid risk or fear failure—I felt the need to fail forward fast.

After risk aversion and fear of failure, indecision is perhaps the most common reason for that innovation-killing standstill we call inertia. It's not easy to act decisively in the midst of chaos, especially when you're under pressure and exhausted. The thing is, any plan is better than no plan, and a good plan executed now is far better than a perfect plan executed too late—WOS leaders never succumb to analysis paralysis. How could you when you're busy innovating and adapting to take advantage of new opportunities?

Note that I'm not advocating knee-jerk responses or acting without thinking here. I'm saying you need to get comfortable with a "good enough" plan (one based upon incomplete information) and develop conviction in the belief that your decisions will improve as you fail forward fast and tap into your resources. You can't allow a fear of failure to keep you from ever starting! Let your intuition guide you (we'll explore how in the next chapter). Your perspective will shift as you act, which is a good thing, and you'll tighten things up as you go. So, after taking a moment to assess the situation, make a decision, use the tools in this book to guide you, and take action as soon as possible, choosing an ethical, positive path forward.

If you're unsure what action to take, try this: Begin by determining your available resources, and then break your old patterns and set a new routine that will reorient your focus and that of your team to the present challenge. These efforts might include conducting research, connecting to others who have experience, and mobilizing your team by delegating preparatory tasks. You may even issue a "warning order," alerting your team to what's coming down the pike. Every business has a battle rhythm—a familiar sequence or process of getting ready to do something big and then doing it—as part of its culture. With each new mission, you'll want a new rhythm to break inertia and get the energy flowing. You might also have new stakeholders whose schedules and priorities must be taken into account.

Let's say, for example, that you're going to launch a new product or service and the contract with your supporting investor is well into negotiations. Part of your warning order could be to task team members with researching the market or brainstorming ideas for a domain name. Where before you may have had operations meetings once a week, now you might plan to meet with your team daily and include your third-party stakeholders in a weekly conference call. Everyone will start shuffling priorities and schedules to accommodate this impending reality if you give them a heads-up. And when those contracts are signed, you'll be poised and ready for action.

WAY OF THE SEAL DRILL

. . . .

Making Decisiveness a Habit

To break things with confidence, you must make decisiveness a habit. Practice with the little things. For example, the next time you're asked for your opinion, such as what movie to see or where to go for dinner, don't just pass the buck and say, "Whatever you want is fine by me." Make a decision immediately. Practice at work, too, especially when beginning a new project. Don't sit on things until you're 100 percent clear on what to do—get everyone moving with a warning order or task key players with gathering information.

Excel in Chaos

When chaos becomes the norm—as when countries, industries, or companies go through periods of rapid change—the human mind is thrown into confusion, immediately seeking homeostasis by looking for remnants of the old, stable system. It will often latch on to any echo of those patterns as evidence that things are normalizing. This can lead to some bad decisions, because these are usually false indicators: When things fall apart, they rarely go back to the old normal, instead settling into a new normal over time. For us, this means even more opportunity as we learn to innovate in rapidly changing environments when everyone else is searching for the past or hunkering down to let the dust settle. In these times, WOS leaders deal with patterns in two primary ways:

- You will avoid old, ritualized patterns in the system, instead seeking new patterns arising out of the chaos. These will point the way to both threats and opportunities for innovation as the system rebalances.

- You will ensure you don't settle into routines of your own, which can elevate your risk, by changing up personal and team routines frequently to keep your perspective fresh while confusing your opponents.

You will benefit greatly by making a friend of chaos and mastering it, even though it can be uncomfortable at first. Remember, the key to breaking through to extraordinary results is to replace an old habit with a new one—make a habit of changing things up constantly and you will override any discomfort you've experienced in the face of chaos or rapid change. This will result in a heightened awareness of new patterns and a strengthened ability to avoid blind spots and break old routines, which will liberate your mind from the restraints of the conventional and allow a strong dose of creativity to flow in. This works well for me. In fact, I get nervous when things stay the same for too long—internal clutter starts to accumulate, stagnating my thinking and encroaching on my creativity. I am much more secure with persistent change because it keeps me on the razor's edge where I must constantly grow to keep pace.

The phrase "routine is the enemy" warns us that the blind spots formed by routine behavior and ritualistic thinking can prevent us from exploiting better opportunities or even lead to danger. However, while some routines stifle and prevent creativity, others free your attention to focus on innovation. Rutted routines that develop from doing the same thing the same way every time—often unconsciously, or at best without deliberate decision-making—are those that stifle creativity. However, when we create rituals around powerful tools for performance and awareness, such as the morning and evening rituals, or when we train the fundamentals common to our missions or critical nodes, such as with your SOPs, then we are grooving peak performance behavior into our subconscious. These are good routines that will help unlock creativity and success.

A subtle pattern to consider is your body and mental posture when making decisions (in other words, your physiology and psychology). Are you slumped, fatigued, negative, or morose? These are weak positions for making an important decision. Change your body posture and charge up your mind with some positive statements before you make that call. How about routines such as using the same meeting room every time you're considering something important? Try changing this environment and you will change the energy and thought patterns before decision time. I am the butt of many good-natured jokes at my training center because I'm constantly changing my office location. Each time I moved, though, I saw the business differently in subtle ways. In fact, I've moved so many times, I finally gave up having an office altogether, which helps me avoid the blind spots and clutter associated with that routine. Not only do I make better decisions, but I figure I am about 25 percent more productive based upon the number of focused, uninterrupted hours I can now spend on writing and other creative projects. Consider breaking your own routines, such as your:

- physical training (visit SEALFIT.com or CrossFit.com for excellent examples)
- food types, quantities, and meal times
- vacation destinations and durations (sorry, but going to the same place at the same time every year is a rut)
- meeting locations for daily, weekly, or annual retreats
- mental and emotional challenges
- playtime activities (going to the same golf course twice a week will not help you fire up new brain cells)

As with so many principles in this book, your efforts to break things are ultimately supported by a deep confidence in your abilities, but where does that confidence come from? Well, you will certainly see an increase in your confidence levels as you work through the practices in this book and come to understand just how much you're truly capable of achieving. But there's also a deeper source of knowing already within you, just waiting for you to tap into it.

WAY OF THE SEAL DRILL

Making Variety a Habit

Make a list of all the routines in your daily and weekly life. What time do you wake? Do you brush your teeth before or after taking a shower? Do you check your e-mail before brushing your teeth? What ritual patterns of thought can you detect? We are good self-deceivers, so why don't you ask your best friend or spouse what your routine habits and thoughts are? Armed with the list, make a parallel list of ways you will break these routines. Get up at a different time every day. Take a different route to work. Do not check e-mail first thing, but only twice a day. Fast for a day or do a juice cleanse. Make a new routine out of shaking things up. This will forge new pathways in your brain, help you to avoid blind spots and rutted thinking, and spice up your life in general. You can easily apply this drill at a team level, also.

★ ★ ★ **EXERCISES** ★ ★ ★

FINDING THE SILVER LINING

This is a great tool for learning from major events and using your insights to ensure that you break things in a deliberate and powerful way rather than repeat them. It's an essential practice when you encounter a "failure," but it's also useful with a win—there's always something to learn. When your event, challenge, or mission is complete, find a quiet place with your journal. Perform deep breathing or Box Breathing to settle yourself. Now, begin by asking yourself "gratitude" questions. You've survived your attempt at, or you've accomplished, something big, so who can you thank and for whom are you grateful? Certainly include yourself, but also think about your family, teammates, mentors, support staff, even your enemy. This starts you off in a positive frame of mind, which is essential for failing forward fast and breaking things effectively.

Next, reflect on your performance. Ask, "How did I do? What did I learn? Did I move the dial on my 20X factor? How can I improve and do even better next time? Was the event worth the time and energy—would I do it again?" Write down your reflections. You don't need to make any decisions, just make sure you write down key thoughts before they are lost or changed through the filter of memory processing.

If, upon reflection, you find aspects of your performance that you are unhappy with, reframe it with a positive lesson. What did you learn? What was the silver lining? Why did it happen the way it did? Whether you won the event or not, you can guarantee that you win the aftermath with how you choose to view what happened and create a positive response to it. This very powerful process can keep you focused on feeding the courage dog and the positive aspects of failure even when you fall on your face.

IDENTIFYING OPPORTUNITIES

This exercise will help you unlock your ability to see potential opportunities that may previously have been hidden. With a notebook in hand, answer the following questions in relationship to your field of interest:

1. Think of any prominent individuals or companies in your domain that have a past focus. Where are they stuck and what beliefs drive their behavior?

2. Think of any prominent individuals or companies in your domain that have a future focus. Where are they stuck in wishful thinking, and what beliefs drive their behavior?

3. Think of any prominent individuals or companies in your domain. How are they present and front-sight focused? What beliefs drive them? What can you learn from them about operating with blazing effectiveness?

When you are satisfied with your answers, sit and practice your Box Breathing for a few minutes, then sit in silence for a few more. When ready, ask yourself:

1. What beliefs do I have that keep me stuck in a past focus, if any?

2. What beliefs do I have that keep me stuck in a future focus, if any? (Remember that you want to look towards the future but operate from the present.)

3. Acknowledging these beliefs and how they limit me, what opportunities open up for me in the present?

4. Is it possible for me to execute on the best one of these opportunities? If not, what is holding me back? What would I need to do to move on it?

Don't forget to journal any insights that come from this exercise.

BUILD YOUR INTUITION

The intuitive mind is a sacred gift and the rational mind
is a faithful servant. We have created a society that honors the
servant and has forgotten the gift.
—ALBERT EINSTEIN, AMERICAN INNOVATOR
AND SCIENTIFIC GENIUS (1879–1955)

Breaking things and then remaking them with your rational mind is only half the equation. Most of your creativity and some of your best ideas will come from the hidden inner mind of your subconscious. Once you learn to harness this powerful intelligence, you will break through to new levels of awareness and accomplishments. I believe these skills will be commonplace in twenty years—let's give you an intuitive leg up on the competition!

You have probably had episodes where you had a bad feeling about a situation, sensed something was going to happen before it did, or had a serious case of déjà vu. If you're like most folks, you probably ignored it. I am proposing you pay close attention to these moments and use them to train your intuition for the benefit of yourself and others. Though many businesspeople might scoff at what some consider "hocus-pocus" (or other choice terms), the modern warrior fields are regaining interest in the study and development of intuition. Beginning in the 1960s, the Soviet military researched arcane psychic techniques such as hypnosis, psychokinesis, precognition, clairvoyance, and ESP. According to declassified CIA reports from the Cold War era, the Soviets had success breaking a man's spine using mental projection (yikes) and also with using clairvoyance to spy on U.S. missile sites. No doubt this spurred the U.S. to initiate studies of its own.

Trojan Horse, an early project conducted with Army Green Berets and Navy SEALs, sequestered a unit to practice aikido (a martial art focused on the ability to detect, merge with, and redirect an opponent's kinetic and potential energies) and meditate for six months. The soldiers were benchmarked for their shooting accuracy, their mental focusing skills, and their subjective sense of stress level. At the end of the test period, the soldiers demonstrated improvements in concentration, accuracy, stress management, and what they described as an "intuitive awareness."

Then there was Stargate, an Air Force–sponsored initiative that used special operators to develop clairvoyance skills they dubbed "remote viewing." Sitting in a room, the subjects could project themselves mentally to a remote location after being provided just a grid reference or place name. Intriguingly, they could relay some precise information through words and drawings of what they saw.

I experienced something similar at an Apache scout–inspired training. The Apache were known as exceptional warriors, and their arduous physical and mental training followed in the same tradition as that of other warriors I respected, such as the Spartans and samurai. I sought out this training to deepen my tracking and awareness skills, particularly in natural environments. Many of the training sessions began with meditation and visualization, including the spirit walk. In this exercise, I examined the beginning of a forest trail without walking up it. Then in the training hall, I projected myself up the trail in my mind. I noted a very prominent feature that looked like a Mormon temple bathed in golden light. Odd, but later, I walked up the real trail and saw what my intuitive mind had seen in cartoon imagery—a solitary massive and beautiful tree, stripped of its bark by a lightning strike and bathed in the golden afternoon sun. I learned from this and other similar experiences that intuitive language is different from rational language: The intuitive mind communicates with us through imagery and sensations, which we can learn to see and understand with practice.

Back on planet Earth, what does all this mean for you? Your intuitive skills are the source of creativity, danger avoidance, and higher levels of thinking and communication. To enhance a "break things" mentality, you must use both the hard skills described thus far in this book as well as the more subtle soft skills described in this chapter. It's time to develop your intuition and use it as a practical tool in your life by:

- expanding your awareness
- strengthening your sensory perception
- uncovering your background of obviousness
- opening up to your inner wisdom

Expand Your Awareness

Let us not look back to the past with anger, nor towards the future with fear, but look around with awareness.

—JAMES THURBER, AMERICAN AUTHOR AND
HUMORIST (1894–1961)

Awareness is the ability to pay close attention to the whole and the parts of a situation simultaneously. We want to be able to take it all in while also maintaining an attention to detail. Intuition development requires us to expand our range of awareness and tap into our subconscious minds at will. The art of using your intuition is to learn by absorbing more information and then accessing it in a sensible form. This skill can help us make better decisions and avoid danger or problems, especially on the fly or in chaotic situations.

Let's combine breathing with how you use your eyes to activate your expanded awareness capabilities. First, there are two ways I teach to use the eyes in my Unbeatable Mind training: Focused Awareness and Relaxed Awareness. The difference is looking intently through your eyes, seeing every detail, versus absorbing information with your eyes, imprinting things your conscious mind may not even be aware of. When you focus your eyes, you focus your mind and shut out distractions. When your goal is to be front-sight focused in the literal sense, this is a valuable skill. However, those distractions may include input critical to a deeper awareness of your situation, including important cues that can inform your quick, decisive actions and give you the confidence to fail forward fast. For instance, when you are focused on one thing you miss the forest for the trees, including patterns that may hold information valuable for your decision-making. So we need a way to stay aware of them as well.

With the Focused Awareness technique, you use your eyes like laser beams, looking through them in a focused manner. It's possible this gaze also projects energy: Recent research by Dr. Colin Ross, author of *Human Energy Fields* and founder of the Colin A. Ross Institute, shows that energy projected out of our eyes can travel hundreds of meters. If you have ever stalked a deer, you know as soon as you look at the deer in a focused manner it will startle and take off. It can feel your energy. When you use your eyes in this manner, your conscious mind is fully engaged in observing and processing information. However, things get even more interesting when we shift out of focus.

Relaxed Awareness is a technique where you defocus your eyes, allowing information to flow through the eyes and into the mind as if they were windows. Your gaze will be soft, with your eyes wide but not looking at anything in particular, similar to using peripheral vision at night. The Apache scouts called this "wide-angle vision" and used it to stalk and deepen awareness. When using our eyes in this manner, the brain dips into a state in which information is passing to and from our subconscious mind. Often this information isn't needed in the moment, but when it's required later in a different context, it comes to us as intuitive gut feelings, inspirational flashes, and creative bursts. Those who learn to imprint upon and then tap into this subconscious wellspring are often seen as geniuses by society—Albert Einstein, for example, was famous for his afternoon naps, often slipping into sleep as he became deeply absorbed in his work of solving equations. Many of his inspirational flashes happened as he fell into or came out of these naps, when his eyes were soft and his brain relaxed. I believe this is what happens to SEALs as they immerse themselves in one challenge after another. You, too, can be a genius, if you apply these principles!

The key to entering a peak learning state that taps into your intuition is to shift between Focused Awareness and Relaxed Awareness, matching a specific breathing pattern and energetic state with each. When activating Focused Awareness, shift your breathing to a deep and powerful inhale and exhale through your nose, as if you are charging your energy stores. In fact, you are doing just that by oxygenating yourself at a cellular level and pumping oxygen-laden blood into your brain. Now you are ready to explode into action. When you don't need to take action but want to absorb as much information as possible, you will shift back into Relaxed Awareness. Here your breathing is also deep, but slower, more rhythmic and controlled, such as with Box Breathing or a similar pattern. Your energetic state is now calm like a still pond. Your eyes go soft into a wide-angle vision as you scan your surroundings, taking it all in.

Imagine a SEAL Platoon on patrol. The SEALs are all using a Relaxed Awareness gaze, their breathing patterns soft and controlled. They are absorbing information, imprinting it at a deep subconscious level. Suddenly, the guy securing the rear feels something tug at his stomach, and his hair bristles. He doesn't wonder what it is; rather, he immediately signals his squad to stop. Instantly all SEALs shift to Focused Awareness. They focus their eyes, looking for clues to the source of danger. Their breathing gets deeper and more forceful as they take

WAY OF THE SEAL DRILL

The KIM Game

The SEALs use a learning tool called the Keep in Memory (KIM) game to develop attention to detail and awareness, and to practice accessing memory through the imprinting process. This is an excellent drill to practice Focused Awareness and Relaxed Awareness. It can be done solo but is more powerful with a team. First, choose twenty random items and place them on a floor or table under a blanket. Do not look at the items. Next, prepare yourself with a few minutes of deep breathing, clearing your mind. When you're ready, remove the blanket and study the items for sixty seconds. Shift between Relaxed Awareness and Focused Awareness to take in details and the whole. Now replace the blanket.

How many of the items can you (or your team) recall? What level of detail do you remember? Repeat this drill until you get really good at the two mental states and remember all the items with nuanced detail. Each time you practice this drill, you will improve your ability to absorb and retain information. Your field of awareness expands, and soon you will be remembering subtle and detailed information wherever you are.

in valuable oxygen. They are now in a heightened, alert state, ready to explode into action.

This looks similar in a business setting. If you're preparing to conduct an important meeting, you're patrolling toward it with Relaxed Awareness, intent on absorbing details and getting a gut feel for important things not in your immediate line of sight. As you near performance time, you shift to Focused Awareness, talking to the team, getting a sense of everyone's agenda and what information needs to be conveyed, ensuring you are in control of the meeting objectives. During the meeting, you'll shift back and forth. For example, you might address a detailed question with Focused Awareness, then relax and allow your awareness to go broad again and use intuitive cues to shape what you're saying and whom you're addressing. Does your gut tell you your current track is losing people's attention or confusing them? Shift gears! Do you get a strong negative vibe from that person in the corner? Ask if he has concerns. Relaxed Awareness provides for more connection with your audience and gets you in the flow.

You can train these states of learning and action with some effort. Ideally, you will learn to shift back and forth at will, accessing an optimal state for learning while also being ready to act on signals from your intuition. Combine this with total commitment and a positive, "fail forward fast" approach, and you will become an unbeatable machine who fearlessly breaks things to create new realities for elite performance.

Your awareness does expand naturally as you age, travel, and take in more experiences. However, you can still be closed to the deeper wisdom within you if you remain in your head all the time. What I would like to do is train you to expand your awareness deliberately by getting out of your head and deepening your connection to your senses and your subconscious genius.

Strengthen Your Sensory Perception

When you start using senses you've neglected, your reward is to see the world with completely fresh eyes.

—BARBARA SHER, AMERICAN SPEAKER AND BESTSELLING AUTHOR OF
WISHCRAFT: HOW TO GET WHAT YOU REALLY WANT (1935–)

If you've ever noticed how good you feel after coming out of nature after an extended stay without your cell phone and laptop, here's the reason why: It's because you slowed down enough to quiet your outer mind, allowing your inner wisdom to poke its head out a bit. Ahhh! Slowing down and engaging the senses fosters a sense of mindfulness. Mindfulness is a practice that leads to a deeper connection with your inner self, a more present state of awareness through which your wisdom can flow. To facilitate this, you want to develop your sensory perception, which means that you take in more information through each of your senses. What are your skin, nose, ears, mouth, and eyes telling you? Are you taking in all the information you can, and would you know it if you were?

When I first entered the working world as an accountant straight out of business school, I was not super-aware in the way I am discussing here. I felt a bit shut off from my senses and intuition, my mind constantly engaged in thinking without remaining receptive to new information. I approached problem solving by either jumping to the conclusion my upbringing and education had primed me to see, or in more thoughtful moments using the scientific method to pose a theory, research and test possibilities, and settle on a solution. I was not alone, as these were and still are typical problem-solving tools for most professionals. As a result, and as many professionals in the same boat have discovered, my decisions were one-dimensional and disconnected from any deeper sense of wisdom or connection to the wisdom of others.

However, when I started practicing meditation at Nakamura's school, things slowly changed. Not only did I experience more with my senses, I developed the ability to "tune in" to the people around me. This paid dividends back at the office because I could connect and communicate more authentically. Rather than immediately reacting with a preprogrammed, automatic response, I could pause and listen with an "empty mind" allowing me to better understand what others thought and felt and to respond accordingly.

Though the SEALs did not deliberately practice mindfulness, our training definitely included similar attributes, such as long periods of forced silence, heightened awareness practices, and mental acuity and toughness drills. I believe these skills, on top of the foundation Nakamura gave me, helped me to earn the Honor Man award. I could sense the ebb and flow of the instructors' battle rhythm for the class and manage my stress by slowing down my breathing and mind, maintaining a calm demeanor in the midst of chaos. By paying very close attention to our instructors' eyes and nuanced facial expressions, I developed the ability to perceive when they were dead serious or just screwing with us.

My developing awareness skills also helped me be a natural leader in spite of the fact that I had no leadership experience when I entered BUDS—for example, I could detect the signs of another student losing his momentum, something I felt in both my heart region and mind when I suddenly knew he would quit, then watched his quit unfold. A growing awareness of my inner dialogue allowed me to better direct my thoughts toward the positive, and I became accustomed to keeping my mouth shut and listening with my whole being, only speaking if asked a direct question or if I had a key insight to offer the team.

As I got into the business world again after the SEALs, my awareness and intuition skills have accelerated due to the daily yoga, martial arts, and meditation training (from which I took an unfortunate hiatus during the CBC debacle!). Nowadays, I would not consider entering an important meeting or phone call without tapping into my senses to see what they have to say. I begin by practicing breath control and stilling my mind, and then I scan my body for clues to my inner state and any messages from my subconscious about what I perceive in others and in the environment. For example, I might intuit that someone feels uneasy or distrustful, and so I would focus on meeting that person's eyes or speaking warmly and directly to them. Or my gut may feel tight, in which case I'd scan for signs that someone isn't being fully honest and exercise greater caution in how much information I share. Often I feel someone's negative, needy energy, and I strive like hell to avoid that person or minimize the impact. I will leave the room when I sense the negativity of a person who has me in his or her radar. If I can't excuse myself politely for some reason, I visualize a protective shield surrounding my body that won't allow any negative energy through. This works well to keep me balanced in meetings.

Develop your sensory perception by tuning into and turning on your senses. Let's add this to your practice tool kit now.

WAY OF THE SEAL DRILL

....

Hone Your Senses

Take a moment to cup your ears and close your eyes. Now just listen and notice what comes up. Your breathing will probably sound like a freight train at first, and you may see images and flashing lights. A moment before you weren't even aware of these internal things! Think of this training as your personal sensory-deprivation tank. (And if you have access to one of those, by all means use it. In fact, any endeavor that plunges you into deep silence—such as scuba diving, rock climbing, parachuting, or cross-country skiing—will heighten this sensory perception.) In the darkness, without noise or visual references, you can get into a deep state of sensory awareness and mindfulness where everything that goes on internally is a big deal. Next, remove your hands from your ears. Just sit quietly and listen. Jot down what you initially hear...then listen more intently. What else do you hear now? Then do it again and yet again. You will note layers upon layers of noises that your brain previously shunted to your subconscious because they were deemed irrelevant.

You can repeat this drill for each of your five senses by following a pattern of deprivation and then intently focusing and going deeper into the isolated sense. For example, what do you see when you shut your eyes or are in total darkness? When you open them, what do you see first? When you look more closely, what do you notice?

Uncover Your Background of Obviousness

It is necessary to the happiness of man that he be mentally
faithful to himself. Infidelity does not consist in believing,
or in disbelieving; it consists in professing to believe
what he does not believe.

—THOMAS PAINE, ENGLISH-AMERICAN POLITICAL
THEORIST AND PHILOSOPHER (1737–1809)

Becoming more aware of our outer, physical environment as well as
our inner, sensory landscape leads to a stronger intuition and dialogue
with our subconscious mind. But how can we be confident in the
messages we receive? When you're in the midst of chaos and need
to take decisive action, how do you know your gut feelings can be
trusted? After all, the mind is incredibly complicated—we've learned
many ways to capture and direct its power in this book, but that necessarily implies that it can be compromised, doesn't it?

Life experiences, especially those from early childhood, can
remain with us a long time. We store the remarkable aspects of an
event—what we need to actively remember in order to survive and
thrive—in our memory centers, while the bulk of the details are
imprinted at a deep, subconscious level. When these imprinted aspects are left to fester, they often solidify into negative or destructive
beliefs, which then drive our behavior in subtle ways for years after
the experience itself. I affectionately call these solidified beliefs your
Background of Obviousness (BOO). That's because they are hidden
in plain sight, obvious to others but not to you. This concept is somewhat similar to the idea of blind spots, except that with BOO we're
talking about unexamined, destructive beliefs and unresolved negative emotions that drive us, as opposed to the deeply rutted patterns
of thought and behavior that create blind spots.

For example, if your mother became extremely upset over minor events—such as your breaking an inexpensive, replaceable vase—then as an adult you may find that you likewise experience perpetual anxiety and frequent outbursts. To you, these feelings and behaviors are completely justified and normal, even if they occur without cause or in disproportion to a triggering event. You might also find yourself going to extremes to avoid confrontation, especially if you think someone is angry at you. Deeply hidden beliefs can cause your subconscious mind to work against your conscious desires in direct and indirect ways. They can sabotage your confidence in your intuition and decision-making, especially when things are tense or chaotic, such as in a "break things" scenario. They can also prevent you from authentically communicating with your teammates, stakeholders, and those whose help or feedback you want to enlist—if you can't hear others over the sound of your own BOO, you're losing out, and so are they.

If you want to succeed at the highest levels, you must align the inner with the outer. This theme repeats itself in this book because it is a base requirement for many of the techniques to work at maximum effectiveness. Often this means you will have to reconnect with or relive your hidden experiences. Now, let's be clear—there's no question that extreme cases (such as perpetual depression, harmful or reckless behavior, and feelings of immobilizing shame) should be handled with an expert therapist. However, I have found through my various awareness-training experiences that we can do much of this work ourselves if we have the right tools. Your mind gym, which you built when exploring Principle 2, is going to be your tool to do your inner work. In it, you have a structure for not only visualizing the future you and your goals, but also for reliving your past in a safe environment. In the mind gym, you can recap your past and tune in with how you developed the beliefs and behaviors you have now, many of which may be holding you back or interfering with your ability to make good decisions.

An example of this is my own work to uncover my BOO. In my teenage years, I felt very detached from others and found it difficult to connect in a deep way. This led to a series of painful relationships in which I couldn't come even remotely close to meeting the emotional needs of the women in my life. This pattern challenged me well into my late twenties—it took the insistence of my therapist girlfriend for me to even start working on it! But because I focused on the behavior and didn't adequately address the root problem, I believe it didn't go away; instead, it transformed and manifested differently. I began to notice that, especially in business settings, I experienced an unusual intensity in conversations when I felt challenged or confronted. For instance, once when I was working at a consulting firm, a more experienced coworker expressed some doubt over one of my proposals. My coworker asked simple, reasonable questions to get me to think about my assumptions—in retrospect, she had some great points and indeed the solution lay in the middle ground. However, I felt as if she were directly challenging my intelligence and competence. My heartbeat increased and my body went on high alert, preparing for a fight. I raised my voice as I answered her questions, taking a far more aggressive tone than the situation called for.

These issues required serious BOO work; I didn't want to be stuck repeating these destructive patterns for eternity! I started seeing a professional therapist and also started developing my own tools. Using the mind gym "Future Me" visualization in reverse, I revisited certain events of my youth—specifically one massive communication breakdown between my parents that I witnessed around age 16, and a few other incidents where my father, under his own BOO spell, lost control over something relatively minor and went into a rage against my brother and me. Going deeper into the fear and guilt associated with these events—my BOO—I soon recognized that the same "self-preservation" energy caused me both to shut down as a young man and to have intense reactions to critical feedback as an adult. I gained great insight into myself through this process, and the self-awareness it unlocked was invaluable in helping me evolve my personality and build better communication skills in both personal and professional relationships.

An effort like this takes great patience and courage. You must push through the resistance to back out of the difficult parts! I'll walk you through the process in the Exercises section at the end of this chapter. The work you do in your mind gym will tune you in to your intuition through your heart and gut so you can feel thoughts rather than just think thoughts. As you develop your intuition, your body will start to alert you when you act out of your BOO and faulty beliefs—it will just feel wrong.

Open Up to Your Inner Wisdom

To think is easy. To act is difficult.
To act as one thinks is the most difficult.
—JOHANN WOLFGANG VON GOETHE,
GERMAN POET AND POLITICIAN (1749–1832)

The stomach is often called the "little brain" because it contains millions of neurons. At a basic level, it can detect whether you have enough blood circulating to digest your food or tell you when you're hungry, but at a more subtle level it's giving you information about what's going on in the rest of your body, which in turn is often a reaction to messages from your subconscious mind. If danger lurks around the corner, or if something just isn't right, part of you knows it and feels it. Your stomach gets the signal and diverts blood to the extremities to prepare them for movement. Your brain may not register the threat, but can feel the tug in your stomach. Trusting your gut is learning how to listen to and acknowledge this information. When your gut feels tight or queasy, you know something is wrong. When it feels good, you can proceed with confidence and calm.

As you work through the practices described in this book, you'll grow more aware and intimate with your subconscious mind. The next stage of this process is to open up a channel for your subconscious mind to communicate with you more clearly—a structure through which your intuition can flow, providing more detailed information than a simple feeling in your gut (though that can be a powerful part of the message, especially in the clutch!), and a tool for clearing out any baggage (read: BOO stuff) that clouds your present decision making. The good news is that you already have this structure and tool—your mind gym! With Principle 2, you learned how to build your mind gym, which is invaluable for enhancing your visualization practice. In the Exercises section at the end of this chapter, you'll learn to use your mind gym in a more receptive way to open up that channel between your conscious and subconscious and to deepen your awareness and intuitive skills. So, ultimately, we are developing the mind gym for two primary purposes: First, the process of building the mind gym and returning to it daily for mental projections and rehearsals enhances your visualization skills and solidifies the internal structure so it has more power for you; second, the mind gym gives your inner awareness and intuition training more structure and makes it more real. Any way you use it, the mind gym is a multiplier for your success.

You can tap into intuitive decision-making most effectively when you have analyzed an important decision in depth and boiled it down to several options but can't get radar-locked on which one is best. In your advanced practice, you may invite an imaginary coach or counselor into your mind gym to provide you with guidance. You can just wait and see who shows up, or this counselor can be someone you know in real life, someone you trusted but who is no longer with you (such as your wise but deceased grandfather) or an important figure from the past (Napoleon Hill talks about Abraham Lincoln as a mental advisor in his seminal work, *Think and Grow Rich*, and José Silva had his children invite an imaginary advisor into their meditation space, as he discusses in his informative book *The Silva Mind Control Method*). The counselor allows you to ask questions of a perceivable person "in here" rather than of something less tangible and "out there." In my experience, this practice has a very positive impact.

When I'm looking for a burst of inspiration or a solution to a challenge, I will often sit for ideas in a quiet room. First, I try to solve the challenge with my analytical mind, including research and thinking through possible solutions using the PROP method (Priorities, Realities, Options, Path) from Principle 3's Exercises section.

When I hit a roadblock, I'll write out my challenge in words or with a drawing. Then I will go to my sit space, perform Box Breathing for a few minutes, and then visit my mind gym to visualize the challenge—sometimes I ask my counselor and sometimes I just sit and wait for images or words to show up on the projection screen I have set up in the gym. This is a form of mindfulness meditation, where I am not actively trying to stop mental activity, rather just watching what bubbles up as my mind settles into an alpha state. A solution often presents itself, sometimes in a few minutes, sometimes in several hours, sometimes later that night in a dream. I've also used this method to help identify opportunities, such as with the Identifying Opportunities exercise from pages 133.

Any type of visualization exercise or practice that calls for you to sit in stillness for answers or ideas is enhanced when you perform it inside your mind gym. Try taking the exercises and drills you've learned thus far and incorporating them into a mind gym meditation to boost their effectiveness and to continue building your mental toughness and intuition.

★ ★ ★ EXERCISES ★ ★ ★

AWAKEN YOUR INTUITION

Using the process described in Principle 2's Exercise section, enter your mind gym and just be present there for a few moments. Express gratitude for having this place to train mentally and for all you have in your life. Next, invite your counselor into the mind gym. You don't have to know who this is in advance; in fact it's better if you don't have a rational concept of who this is—just see who shows up! When I did this an old man with long hair and the strength of a warrior—who I believe was an Apache scout—showed up. He continues to be my counselor to this day. When your counselor arrives, thank him or her, invite them to sit with you (I have a dedicated spot in the room for mine), and then ask your question. Don't expect to start having a conversation right away, though many of my students admit to having rich and rewarding conversations with their counselors, who impart knowledge that was previously unknown to them. Instead, you may receive images, a flood of emotion, or just a strong sense of the right answer. When you're finished, be sure you thank your counselor for his or her time.

This exercise certainly requires an element of trust, but once you get comfortable with your counselor, my bet is you will develop a nice partnership that will serve you for the rest of your life. I recommend keeping a notepad or recorder handy. Keep it near your bed, especially after asking a question or posing a problem in your mind gym, in case your answer comes during a dream or strikes you in that twilight before you fall asleep and while you're waking up.

In a tight spot, if you've analyzed a situation and are unsure of the way forward, try carefully constructing a simple yes or no question that will answer the issue. State it positively and affirm that you are

150

asking your inner self for the good of all concerned. Feel a burning desire to know the best answer to this question; don't waste energy ammo on frivolous questions or on issues you don't really care about. Then take your question into your mind gym.

For example, after reading this book, you may feel moved to re-structure your team. Let's say you're debating whether to hire a new VP of marketing. Go into a quiet room, sit down, and visit your mind gym. Once in your mind gym, ask the question (or ask your counselor if you have one) "Is so-and-so the right person for this role?" As soon as you ask the question, pay close attention to any images, emotions, or sensations that arise. If nothing comes up, end your session (don't forget to always thank your counselor for his or her presence) and then continue to pay close attention for the next twenty-four hours. Often you'll immediately feel a tug or tightening in your belly, which means "No!" A sudden release or an expansive, relaxed feeling means "Yes!" You may also see a symbol or image in your mind. Again, pay attention to the quality and feelings associated with the image. If you see a train wreck . . . well, you get the picture!

Some advanced tips to help ensure the effectiveness of your mind gym practice:

1. Before you enter your mind gym to visualize a goal, you must be very clear on what you desire and articulate it in positive terms as if it had already happened. Then you must infuse the visualization with the belief that the process is helping you achieve that goal.

2. You must be consistent between what you seek to achieve in your visualization and what your BOO beliefs are telling you. If you visualize a financial goal, but in your subconscious mind you tell yourself you can't afford it or don't deserve it, then you will cancel out the positive benefits of the visualization. You must eliminate any beliefs that contradict your desired outcomes before embarking on the visualization. In this case, you will

want to use the mind gym to uncover your BOO and also to plant seeds of worthiness before returning to the work of seeing, believing, and making it happen.

3. You must develop the subtle ability to recognize and receive information from the subconscious. This is hard at first, but will come with practice and with experience if you approach the mind gym technique with openness. The process of inviting a "counselor" into your mind gym can help.

4. You will want to take action on synchronicities that occur and doors that open up to you after completing a mind gym practice. Once you open up to your inner wisdom and learn to control the imprinting of your subconscious mind through positive visualization, insights will flow forth more easily, and the universe often seems to conspire with your subconscious for the win!

CLEARING OUT YOUR BOO

In a practice they called "recapitulation," the legendary Toltecs were said to require their budding warriors to undergo this process for every major event in their lives all the way back to their birth! I won't ask you to take it to that extreme, but it's crucial that warriors following the Way of the SEAL operate with true self-awareness, unimpeded by their own hang-ups and negative mental and emotional baggage. I recommend you start a regular BOO practice as soon as your visualization and sacred silence skills will support it (i.e. when you're able to maintain a clear, still mind for at least five minutes and can bring some sensory detail into your visualizations without getting distracted by mental chatter), beginning with once per week and then perhaps increasing or decreasing frequency depending on the intensity of your BOO. It's also a good idea to include this exercise as part of annual "checkup from the neck up" with a professional therapist even after you've cleared out your initial bulk of negative emotional baggage. I'll offer some guidance on evaluating your progress in a moment, but first, the exercise.

Here goes: Use the same process as on page 54 to quiet yourself and enter your mind gym. Once there, state out loud or mentally your intention to explore your BOO. Now, instead of projecting onto your mental screen an image of your desired future, allow your mind to scan back in time to events in your life that were uncomfortable, distasteful, or flat-out painful. If there's a specific incident you want to revisit, you can go straight there. Otherwise, just allow whatever comes up to become your point of focus. (Alternatively, you can begin with a particular behavior or event in mind). When your mind settles on a time and place, let the images on the screen slow to a crawl and then merge with the imagery as if you had traveled back in time. Embody the experience with all your senses as though you were living through it again, right now.

Note any sensations and emotions that arise in your body, especially noting where they show up and what level or degree of discomfort they cause. These responses are clues that will help you identify where negative emotional energy is stored and how intense it is. The location becomes the point of focus for your awareness during the remainder of the exercise. For instance, you may experience a sick feeling in the pit of your stomach, or you may notice your heart racing as your chest tightens. The intensity will indicate the severity of the issue. Rate how intense your response is on a scale of 1 to 10, 1 being not very intense and 10 very intense. If a response elicits a rating of 10, this issue affects you very deeply and you will need to spend a lot of time working on it. If it elicits a rating of 2, you can deal with it more quickly, then move on.

Next, bring the younger version of you into the present to meet the current you in your mind gym. In other words, if the painful event happened when you were 10 years old, visualize your 10-year-old self standing before you. When you can clearly see your younger self, talk to him or her about the inciting event. Say that everything is okay now—it wasn't their fault, it's over and all is forgiven. Tell him or her that it's okay to release the pain and let the upset feelings go.

You may even want to imagine hugging your younger self or offering comfort in some other way. Finally, before you gratefully say goodbye to your younger self, ask him or her to integrate with your current self. You may receive agreement or you could even go so far as to visualize your two bodies merging into one.

If this all sounds silly to you, just do the best you can. Trust me, it is a powerful exercise. When I did this for a painful incident in my own life, my younger self felt so relieved, he jumped up and down and started doing cartwheels!

The final step in this exercise is to bring the original event back up on the screen in your mind gym and again visualize your younger self and any other involved parties. Let the scene play out, noticing any differences in imagery or how you feel. Does your younger self appear less stressed? Is his or her body language more powerful and confident? Do the other parties to the event look less intimidating or angry? Bring your awareness to the location in which you identified stored emotion—how does it feel now? Rate the intensity again and compare to your initial rating. You should feel a decrease, even if only a little. You will want to repeat this process for this specific event until your younger self appears whole and healthy, the third parties no longer pose a threat, and your stored negative emotions have dissipated (meaning the intensity now ranks a 1 or 0).

It's very possible that some BOO issues will be too deeply rooted or scary for you to get at yourself, so you may need a trained therapist to assist you. I recommend you seek someone trained in EMDR (www.emdr.com), a therapeutic process that approaches BOO work through the nervous system. FOR YOUR SAFETY: If you were severely physically or emotionally abused in childhood, do not try to "self-medicate" using this drill without the support of a professional.

You may wonder what issues are candidates for this exercise. My hunch is that you already have a sense of your BOO challenges. Everyone's experiences and personalities are different, but to identify some of your possible BOO issues, start by looking at obvious personality traits or reactions that get in the way of optimal health, performance, relationships, and general happiness, such as extreme or unreasonable anger, bullying impulses, chronic negativity (about yourself or the world in general), depression, or unhealthy sexual behavior. If you are courageous enough, ask your spouse, best friend, or doctor for insight—often others can see the influence of our BOO better than we can.

AUTHENTIC COMMUNICATION

This practice is very powerful for building your intuition muscles as you expand your awareness with regard to both how other people express their feelings non-verbally and how you do the same. The essence is to maintain a Focused Awareness on what your communication partner is saying, while maintaining a Relaxed Awareness on your thoughts and feelings in response to what he or she is communicating. Note that you will get better at this internal awareness as a natural outgrowth of deepening your sensory awareness and emotional resilience. Then, when you feel the need to speak (which, incidentally will be much less often when you do this practice routinely), you will pause before you respond, then open your mouth to speak only if:

- what you have to say is truthful
- what you have to say adds value and is helpful to the conversation
- what you have to say is positive and comes from a place of respect and genuine concern for the other party

THINK OFFENSE, ALL THE TIME

Do not go where the path may lead;
go instead where there is no path and leave a trail.
—RALPH WALDO EMERSON, AMERICAN ESSAYIST AND POET
(1803–1882)

It's typical for most people and groups, especially businesses, to adopt a defensive mind-set. When things go wrong, they hunker down and prepare to ride out the storm. My intention is that you will never be caught in a defensive mental posture again—you can't hope for the best, and then wait to see what happens. Instead, you will scan the field, prepare for the worst with contingencies, and take action at the first sign of opportunity. You will always be prepared to take action, no matter the circumstances, knowing and expecting you will win every time you step foot in the arena. To accomplish this, you must retune your attitude to a "think offense, all the time" mind-set.

Human interaction within our own teams, families, and communities is difficult enough, but when it cuts across cultural lines as we interact with other teams, families, and communities it can be downright messy. Misunderstanding in personal relationships, conflict in business, and war between nations are part of the human experience and will be for a long time to come. Though seeking a win-win-win solution at the personal, team, and organizational levels is important and laudable, it's also understandably difficult at the geopolitical and multinational company level. That is why I believe the unconventional tactics, strategies, and tools used by the SEALs, supercharged with an offensive mind-set, make a valuable tool kit for leaders operating on the global stage. And since increasing globalization puts us all on a global stage, these skills will be valuable for small and midsize businesses as well.

When faced with the mess of conducting business in an environment that looks more like a battlefield than a boardroom, I say, don't settle for the hope that you will win—stack the deck in your favor. The advanced skills of winning with an offensive mind-set include:

- developing unwavering confidence
- sharpening your awareness
- doing the unexpected
- leading with rapid execution

Whether at home, at work, or even out having fun, how you think and deal with opportunities and threats will determine whether you are the victor or victim. Destiny can strike anytime, anywhere. For success in the Way of the SEAL, you must develop your winning attitude and become a more offense-oriented leader.

Develop
Unwavering Confidence

The best way to predict your future is to create it.
—Abraham Lincoln, U.S. President
(1809–1865)

You might recall from our discussion about emotional resilience that while at SEAL Team THREE, I went through the SCARS program—300 hours of aggressive training in offensive mind-set and hand-to-hand combat delivered over thirty days. This was my first "self-confidence course." My martial arts training had given me so many valuable tools and experiences, but I knew I still had a ways to go. The lead instructor, Jerry Peterson, said to me, "Mark, you need to unlearn that karate language. If you block, you're dead." The defensive nature of karate training had burdened me with defensive language, which inadvertently trained my body to respond slowly or not at all to real threats and opportunities. I saw now that I needed to change my language to change my behavior.

This goes deeper than just feeding the dog of courage and remaining positive. You can be positive and still use weak words, rendering you powerless. When I used words such as defense, block, and deflect, my mind sent signals to my body to retreat, protect, and slow down. Words stimulate imagery, so the images in my mind were also defensive and weak. Without realizing it, I had undermined my ability to remain totally committed.

This was a big surprise—though I had a clearly defined set point and the physical strength, front-sight focus, and mental toughness to get through SEAL training, I was not yet programmed to win. I understood the concept of positive self-talk in the clutch, but hadn't expanded that to eradicate weak, defensive language from my vocabulary or replace it with stronger, offense-oriented words and phrases. If that sounds like you, too, let's drill.

WAY OF THE SEAL DRILL

Change Your Words, Change Your Attitude

Make an honest assessment of the language that you use on a daily basis. Do you use negative or "slow down" words? Note the imagery that the words in the first column of the list below conjure up in your mind. Now compare these with the images conjured up by the words in the second column. Major difference, right? Write down any other defensive or negative words you use on a regular basis and write a positive word or phrase to replace it. Repeat the imagery exercise with your own two columns to make sure you're on the right track. Practice using the new language daily and journal your findings every week. Keep at this until it becomes a new habit and second nature.

Defend	Attack
Good	Great
Block	Strike
Retreat	Pounce
Can't	Will
Try	Do
Failed	Learned
Maybe	Definitely

Tap Your Mental Toughness

Jerry hammered into us the need to maintain a positive mind and use offense-oriented language and tactics to maintain the upper hand, keeping our attackers off balance and in defensive mode. When he demonstrated on us as test dummies, anything that looked or even appeared defensive was met with "violence of action" (a SEAL term for controlled aggression applied to a military problem); he would cut through us like we were made of butter, proving how a defensive mindset can slow you down. He was also trying to get a rise out of us so we could face our emotional baggage and bring it under better control.

Often all thirty of us lined up on the sand berm in front of the SEAL compound and fought each other up and down the line for an hour straight, no breaks. When we wanted to stop, the instructors pushed us to keep going. One instructor was a SEAL named Lew Hicks. Lew was particularly aggressive, and he liked demonstrating on me, I think, because my skills developed fast and so I provided him with a nice challenge. By day twenty, I was fluid and much more confident and offensive in my movements and style. Lew decided to test me by cutting me down to size over the course of a few supertough fights and, sure enough, he triggered an emotional response. Frankly, I wanted to kill him. Just as I was about to let loose my impressive skills on him (a losing proposition, I might add), I heard my mentor Grandmaster Nakamura's voice in my head echoing Jerry's advice: "The karateka (read: warrior) must not lose control of his mind and emotions." I was able to bring my emotions back into check using my mental toughness techniques (such as the process described on page 100) and continue the training. Noticing my renewed confidence and calmness, Lew soon lost interest and moved on to torment another student.

Over the final ten days, I made a point of being as offensive-minded as possible while also tapping into my mental-toughness toolbox to maintain emotional control. These two must go hand in hand: An offensive mind-set is the vehicle that allows you to focus your emotional energy, in a controlled manner, toward the target. A trained and intense emotional state, in a fight, can look a lot like rage to an untrained eye and is very intimidating. However, it's not rage; it's controlled energy. I've worked to develop more emotional control and resilience ever since.

With an unwavering confidence honed through offense-style language and powered by emotional mastery and mental toughness, you are well on your way to a SEAL-like offensive mind-set. But the human brain is extraordinarily complex and has many mechanisms for survival that can create potential mental traps. These traps can trip you up and derail your efforts, no matter how offense-oriented you feel.

Avoid Mental Traps

Thinking offensively requires you to make quick judgments, and unwavering confidence requires that we can trust these judgments. However, we all suffer from certain mental traps that cause us to form these snap judgments poorly. Mental traps turn critically decisive choices into land mines of faulty perceptions. When you know where the land mines are, you can avoid them and thus move forward with the strength and rock-solid certainty of a SEAL.

Perhaps the most common mental trap is "confirmation bias." In a nutshell, as soon as you believe something to be true, you will seek confirmation to support your view and will shut out evidence to the contrary. Confirmation bias is just one of many mental traps we fall into, disrupting attempts at good decision making. Other common mental traps to look out for include a tendency to:

- **Avoid things you doubt, rather than investigate them.** A good example of this is yoga. For years, most American men thought yoga was only for women, wimps, or odd people who wore towels on their heads. In reality it is an incredibly advanced personal-development program that will kick your ass and change your life. I have helped break this myth by teaching my SEALFIT yoga to thousands, including many Navy SEALs.

- **Feel you owe something to people who give you something.** Consider the Hare Krishna at the airport handing out flowers or charities sending you complimentary address labels. We act on these obvious manipulations because we feel beholden to reciprocate after we get something free.

- **Believe that if something is good for someone you know, then it must be good for you, too.** This form of confirmation bias shows up as "herd mentality" when it plays out on a large scale. While good for business in the form of referrals, it can adversely affect you if the referral is the wrong fit (if you and the referrer have dissimilar needs or characters, you're unlikely to be satisfied by the same things) or if the herd is heading off the cliff toward a Ponzi scheme.

- **Wait for social proof before acting.** This is herd mentality in reverse—many people just won't take action on something new until a majority is doing it, such as with new technology or fashion trends. You can miss great opportunities with this tendency. Warren Buffett is famous for saying that the time to invest in the market is when everyone else is getting out, and the time to get out is when everyone else is buying in.

- **Cling to things once you have them.** This trap causes people to ride a failing stock or business idea to the bottom. People who fall prey to this mental trap will never let go of something—even if there is a good reason to do so.

- **Inflate the value or veracity of authority figures' ideas, thoughts, and decisions.** This tendency reflects a desire to link causality to our beliefs. Unfortunately, the causal link between time in a job or rank, and good decisions, is statistically irrelevant. Always question authority!

For some great supplemental reading on mental traps and models to help you avoid them, I highly recommend the groundbreaking book *Thinking, Fast and Slow* by Daniel Kahneman, who won the 2002 Nobel Prize in Economic Sciences. Also check out the work of Charlie Munger, the vice-chairman of Warren Buffett's company, who's worth more than $30 billion himself. He's given many insightful speeches on this topic. If brilliant billionaires like Buffett and Munger don't fully trust their own minds, surely you and I should be wary as well.

Activate Your Radar

The ultimate value of life depends upon awareness and the
power of contemplation rather than upon mere survival.

—ARISTOTLE, GREEK PHILOSOPHER AND
POLYMATH (384 BCE–322 BCE)

In my twenties, I mistook bravado for confidence. As an MBA and
CPA with a newly minted black belt and on my way to the SEALs,
I thought I was the cat's meow. Then one night, while on leave from
Officer Candidate School during winter break, I learned my next lesson. On New Year's Eve in Lake Placid, New York, where my family
had a vacation home, my brother Brad and I went into a bar around
closing time—a little later than we needed to be out. My head was
shaved, and I likely projected an attitude of "feeling special" that
would have annoyed the locals (these days it would annoy me, too).
As I ordered a drink, I noted the pretty bartender and smiled at her,
asking her name. To be honest, I'd just been released from what felt
like prison for a month (OCS didn't allow much socializing . . . actually none at all) and was looking for someone to hold hands with
besides my brother. She looked unimpressed, though, as she shouted,
"Jimmy, got another one!" I had no idea who she was speaking to or
what that meant, but in retrospect, she clearly wasn't interested.

Suddenly a small, agile guy, in his late twenties flew at me from
behind and wrapped his arms around my neck in a tight noose. Between the late hour and my eagerness for some female attention, saying I'd let my guard down would be an understatement. The attack
stunned me; some part of my brain hoped the whole thing was a mistake. Finally, as I began to black out, I started struggling with the guy.
Too late. I passed out on the floor, and if my brother hadn't come back
from the bathroom right then, I could have been killed. When I came
to a moment later, I got up off the floor and stood there feeling like a
fool. I saw my brother in a tense standoff with my attacker. I grabbed

Brad by the arm to avoid a repeat, and then dragged him out of there. That moment was a turning point in my life. Until then I honestly thought I could defend myself against anyone in any situation—heck, I even had a black belt in karate. As I reflected on the situation while nursing my bruised neck over the next two weeks, I realized my karate training was just the beginning. In fact, awareness—not just being able to throw a punch—held more value as a skill for avoiding danger or a confrontation, and for surviving when you're suddenly in one despite your best efforts. I understood that true, unwavering confidence would come when I developed the ability to remain aware of my surroundings at all times, so I would never be caught off guard and stunned into immobility again.

In the Teams, we use the Cooper Color system (named after Lieutenant Colonel Jeff Cooper, who used it for marksmanship training) to sharpen our awareness like an internal radar. The colors each represent different states of awareness, from ignorance to violent action. White is a complete lack of awareness of one's surroundings. Yellow represents an alert posture, scanning for threats and opportunities. Orange is an escalation to the preparatory stage, ready to fight or crank it up as necessary. Finally, red represents total commitment to action . . . take the shot, make the move.

SEALs learn to stay at the Yellow level as a baseline so we can act with speed and surprise if we spot an enemy. I recommend that you do the same. Since you aren't likely facing life-or-death situations, what kind of threat or enemy do you need to be aware of? Your enemy is your competition, whether that's an individual gunning for your job or an organization whose product competes with yours in a specific marketplace. A threat could be anything from warning signs that the marketplace is changing, to your competitor's latest product beating yours to the shelves, to a global financial meltdown that could mean layoffs or even bankruptcy for your company.

The "Yellow Radar" exercise at the end of this chapter and the integration of concepts like navigating gaps for opportunity will develop your situational awareness while strengthening your inner awareness skills, as well. But, like a SEAL, you must learn to act aggressively and rapidly when you become aware of the threats facing you. You must also take advantage of opportunities by innovating and adapting, doing the unexpected to keep your competition off balance.

Do the Unexpected

Rules are made for people who aren't willing to make up their own.
—CHUCK YEAGER, RETIRED BRIGADIER GENERAL,
U.S. AIR FORCE (1923–)

With Principle 6, we learned how to break things so we can remake them better. Now we want to remake our very thought processes and our way of looking at the world so that we can do the unexpected in order to get unconventional (read: extraordinary) results.

Doing the unexpected fundamentally asks you to look at things from a different angle than everyone else. When you train yourself to see what others don't see, then you can unlock your innate creativity. People generally expect that others will follow "the rules," which may literally be rules as in a competition or may be somewhat more abstract as in cultural norms. So, it naturally follows that doing the unexpected often means breaking the rules. SEALs have a blank slate "all options are on the table" approach: We don't follow the enemy's rules or even our own rules if they are archaic or broken; we don't stick with the status quo and don't like to do things the way they were done in the past.

A key attribute of an unconventional mind-set is the ability to know when, and when not, to apply it. Breaking the rules within ethical boundaries is a unique, advanced-level skill that allows SEALs to exploit opportunities where others don't expect them to be or where they aren't even looking. When an individual, culture, or system gets stuck doing the same thing the same way all the time, there is tremendous opportunity to be had by finding a way to sneak around or through their ruts. The more extreme the circumstances, such as outright war, the more extreme the rule-breaking. When I went through BUDS, the instructors were fond of saying "Divine, if you ain't cheatin', you ain't tryin'!" They weren't asking my teammates and me to become liars and cheats but to think unconventionally by pushing the envelope around the edges of accepted behavioral rules and norms.

Let me be perfectly clear that I am not recommending unethical behavior but rather unconventional behavior. Can there be a fine line? Yes. SEALs also learn a strict ethical foundation (recall the SEAL Ethos on page 16) that allows them to be clear on what rules are appropriate to break and when it's appropriate to break them.

What Rules Should Be Broken?

By this point, you have a strong ethical foundation in the form of your stand and principles, which together create a powerful set point keeping your feet in the sand and your eyes on the correct path forward. Given that, what rules are the ones to break? The answer isn't simple, because in truth it's very situational. In general, the rules to break are those that:

- represent weak patterns of behavior, perhaps built upon outdated models of thinking or structures that are hampering your performance (such as expectations for how things are done set by company "old timers" who haven't embraced new technologies that could improve productivity or effectiveness)

- blind you or your competition or inadvertently constrain perfectly good options for getting the job done (like the prevailing military opinion that civilian equipment isn't appropriate for Spec Ops—a "rule" that SEAL Team THREE's Commander McRaven broke when he decided to use blacked-out, sound-muted Jet Skis for tactical insertions in the 1990s)

• are outdated, impractical, unethical in our worldview, that go against internationally accepted standards, or that are flat-out stupid and easy to exploit with little consequence (for example, an Afghan woman seeking a job where she will work side by side with men is breaking the rules of her home culture, though few employers in non-Muslim countries would uphold this restrictive standard)

Retired SEAL Lance Cummings, now my SEALFIT Director of Training, tells of the time his platoon penetrated a Marine installation to test its security and readiness. The Marines, aware of the test, doubled down on their security protocols. Cummings and his men anticipated this move, so they went to the local fire department for support. Later that evening, they drove right through the base gates in their newly commandeered fire truck, sirens blaring. The Marines had no idea they'd just been duped—because the Gate Guards aren't taught to break any rules but to enforce them.

The SEALs broke the cultural rule of the Marines that emphasizes order and discipline and rejects the circumventing of accepted norms. The SEALs cared most about mission accomplishment. Their unconventional methods served them well, even if it embarrassed a few Marine Gate Guards.

In a similar story, during my 2004 deployment to Iraq as a Reserve officer, I learned that the Marine USSOCOM detachment, assigned to SEAL Team ONE, had arrived with vehicles built for desert mobility. I wondered how they would meet their mission since the trucks weren't the slightest bit suitable for the urban, high-bomb-threat environment the Marines faced in Baghdad. Unfortunately, they were looking powerless for the six months it would take the Marines' procurement system to get them new armored Humvees, because they couldn't even leave the compound in the vehicles they had. The detachment would be back in the States by then with egg on their faces.

Fortunately for the Marines, the SEALs didn't mind breaking the rules to ensure their teammates could fight the war as intended. Upon learning of the situation at the daily operations meeting, the commanding officer turned to Warrant Officer Johnson, whom he'd affectionately dubbed his "asset reallocation specialist," and said simply, "Bart, just get it done. You know the deal." Warrant Officer Johnson smiled and started giving instructions to a junior SEAL. A week later, I saw ten Humvees roll through the gate. The Marines were stunned and grateful as they joined the SEALs in armoring them up. The commander made sure the favor was returned in triplicate to the National Guard unit that "donated" the vehicles to the Marines.

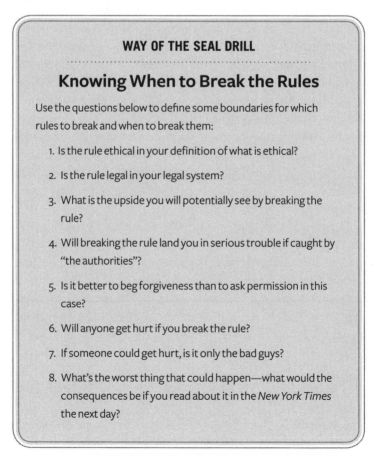

WAY OF THE SEAL DRILL

Knowing When to Break the Rules

Use the questions below to define some boundaries for which rules to break and when to break them:

1. Is the rule ethical in your definition of what is ethical?

2. Is the rule legal in your legal system?

3. What is the upside you will potentially see by breaking the rule?

4. Will breaking the rule land you in serious trouble if caught by "the authorities"?

5. Is it better to beg forgiveness than to ask permission in this case?

6. Will anyone get hurt if you break the rule?

7. If someone could get hurt, is it only the bad guys?

8. What's the worst thing that could happen—what would the consequences be if you read about it in the *New York Times* the next day?

What rules were broken? Well, mainly those guiding the procurement systems of both the Marine Corps and the National Guard. However, any senior enlisted combat vet will smile and say, "No big deal, happens all the time in war." That is my point. The SEALs broke the rules by bypassing the system, the Marines broke the rules by accepting and using the Humvees, and the National Guard broke the rules by signing the assets over to the SEALs in the first place. But no one cared because there was a war going on, and the rules, built for peacetime, were hampering performance. Ultimately, the context of a situation will be the deciding factor for which rules to bend and how far to bend them. In this combat scenario, no one was going to challenge the warrant officer because what he did was critical for a high-priority mission. In peacetime, however, his actions might have landed him in the brig.

Rules to Break Right Now

Unconventional thinking also requires us to investigate the rules driving our personal behavior and to break those that don't serve us any longer. When we do, it will spark our creativity and lead to innovation and superior results. To start shifting you into an offensive mind-set, let's look at some common rules and explore how we can approach them in an uncommon manner. Break these rules and you'll be well on your way to greater success.

Rule to Break No. 1: Become a Great Multitasker

In case you didn't receive the news flash, the myth of multitasking for efficiency has been busted. However, it still has a powerful hold over us, especially with the introduction of the iPhone and other smart technologies that allow our brains to distract us with so many cool things in lieu of whatever we are supposed to focus on right now. Though it is possible for your brain to handle multiple processing sequences, such as chewing gum and rubbing your belly, you can only truly focus on one thing at a time. According to Gary Keller, author of *The One Thing*, multitasking leads to more mistakes due to the mental tendency to favor new information over old; a distorted sense of time, taking far longer than necessary to accomplish the important things; lost time as you bounce back and forth between tasks (Keller estimates a 28 percent loss of your workday!); reduction of the brain power committed to each task, risking weaker performance on all tasks. Finally, it's interesting to note that Keller's research found multitaskers are less happy than those who learn to focus on one thing at a time.

Rule to Break No. 2: Nice Guys Finish Last

I am a very nice guy, but if you saw me facing a new class at the start of Kokoro Camp you probably wouldn't say so. In those moments, a casual passerby could easily mistake me for a monster even though there isn't a negative thought in my head. Focused determination is often mistaken for stern, cold, or even mean. That's fine: It is okay to be both nice and intensely focused, determined to win. When in those moments of intense focus, everyone who matters (those who actually know you) knows you have your game face on and are not intending to be short or mean, even if you may appear that way. "Nice" in our society and organizations typically means you go overboard to get along; you give in to peer pressure, kowtow to the boss, consider a tie a win, and allow "B" players to stay on the team to avoid making them feel bad. These are all recipes for mediocrity. You don't have to be mean to win, and nice people don't have to finish last.

Rule to Break No. 3: More Is Better

This is actually true in very few cases, yet it is a dominant belief in our society. More responsibility is given by moving someone up the ladder, even though doing so may not be in the best interests of the individual or organization. Bigger business is seen as better by "the markets" even though the bigger an organization is, the more divorced it gets from its original mission and its customers, investors, and stakeholders. The more you stack your to-do list with tasks, commitments, projects, and leadership roles, the less meaningful work you will actually get done. A better idea is to apply the KISS principles and then do only those things aligned with your major life or work goals. Same is true at an organizational level: Strive to do fewer things better by narrowing down your daily actions to one to three critical tasks that will move the dial toward your purpose-aligned targets.

Rule to Break No. 4: Fight Fair!

Do you think that drunk at the local watering hole is going to restrain from taking cheap shots when he charges you? Can you count on a coworker in competition with you to highlight favorable details about your project or results when she makes a presentation to your bosses? The very act of fighting (read: competition) is unfair, so there is no such thing as a fair fight. If you must fight—whether real fisticuffs or a boardroom brawl—you must be offensive and unconventional in your approach. This means you are aggressive and leverage surprise and speed to defeat your competitors. However, you can be intensely competitive while at the same time supercooperative. In the SEALs, we would train daily together—a very cooperative, team-building endeavor. However, each training session turned into a barn-burning competition to stimulate intensity and our winning spirit. The best businesses have this same balance between competition and cooperation. This balance requires deep confidence in your skills and the personal power you bring to the table so you can help others without feeling as if you were risking your own win in the process.

Rule to Break No. 5: Always Tell the Truth

I can hear the howls already. But seriously, who reading these words has never told a lie? My point here is that it's important to learn what truth to tell to whom—the whole, part, or none. Often it's a good idea to filter truth to protect others or to deceive an opponent. Sometimes it's best to keep your mouth shut and be thought a fool than to open it and be proved as one. An example of this is if you have information that could be damaging to your leader's reputation. It may be true she slipped up and did something stupid, but that doesn't define who she is as a person, and it's not your job to drive the stake in further. If asked whether you knew about the situation, you may consider leaving well enough alone and holding your tongue. On the other hand, sometimes it's better to speak up than allow someone to take advantage of you. An example of this scenario is when you know a teammate is doing something that could seriously impair the team's ability to accomplish its mission. In this case, your loyalty to the team and organization trumps your loyalty to the teammate. Instead of lying (or keeping mum) to protect him, you could tell him you have already talked to the boss and the boss will be more lenient if he confesses himself. With this little lie, you'll get him the help he needs without jeapordizing the team or the mission. Or, if the situation really warrants it, you could take the truth to the right corners. Sometimes being virtuous means making hard choices.

Rule to Break No. 6: Eat Three Square Meals a Day

I haven't talked much about nutrition in this book, but as a leader seeking extraordinary results, you must understand that how you fuel your body and mind is critical. I believe nutrition accounts for at least 50 percent of your performance. The "three square meals" myth evolved because of industrial-age work schedules, but the human body is designed for as-needed fueling. I eat when I'm hungry throughout the day, which leaves my valuable lunch hour free. For elite leaders, lunch is "training time" where you can get a workout in, practice your WOS skills, take a walk, or otherwise do something that looks nothing like work to refresh your mind, body, and spirit. As for what to eat, I like modified paleo and vegetarian diets: Ditch sugar and carbs from processed grain products (cereal, pasta, and bread), and rely on protein from lean meat or vegetarian sources like nuts, carbs from veggies and fruit, and fat from wholesome sources such as avocados and olive oil. Less is often more, but occasionally gorging yourself is good to confuse the body and remind you how good it feels to eat less. My personal rule of thumb is to behave 80 percent of the time, and then cheat like hell the other 20 percent—life's too short to deny yourself, and this will give you something to look forward to. For a more in-depth discussion of nutrition, check out my book *8 Weeks to SEALFIT*.

Rule to Break No. 7: Be Real, All the Time

I want you to be real with your intimate team—authenticity is critical in a leadership role. But most folks have difficulty being authentic with people they don't know well. Shyness and an inability to be yourself in front of others is a liability for a leader, so sometimes you have to fake it till you make it. These are times when you simply must act the part. Studying the art of acting gives you the skills to engage your audience in a way that isn't natural for most people. To be a good actor, you must get out of your shell and in touch with your full range of emotions, then learn to tap into those emotions at will and display them in dramatic ways. Try an acting or public speaking class (Toastmasters is a great resource) to improve your performance when interacting with a new team or less familiar agents of your organization.

Rule to Break No. 8: Nothing Good Comes Free

In today's marketplace, the real commodity is trust. How do we earn customers' or clients' trust? By helping them achieve their goals without asking for anything in return. Consumers increasingly expect this in the form of things like free white papers, free samples, and free consultations. And what you offer has to have real value, too—it won't work if you offer something they can't actually use or implement. The more value your free offer has to customers, the more likely they are to invest their hard-earned money with you by purchasing your products or services, and the more likely they are to tell their friends, which taps into the power of the elusive buzz. Most will never become customers, but among the minority of those who love your content you will find a growing and loyal following of lifetime patrons. At SEALFIT.com I give away more free content than I could have ever imagined doing even five years ago. I love doing it and have built a base of over a hundred thousand enthusiastic followers as a result.

Execute with Velocity and Agility

Let a man in a garret but burn with enough intensity
and he will set fire to the world.
—ANTOINE DE SAINT-EXUPERY,
FRENCH AUTHOR AND AVIATION PIONEER (1900–1944)

In his book *Theory of Spec Ops*, Commander William McRaven, who was my commanding officer at SEAL Team THREE, identified five principles common to successful special operations throughout history: purpose, repetition, security, surprise, and speed. Twenty years later, as the admiral in charge of all U.S. Spec Ops forces, he followed these principles to the letter for the capture of Osama Bin Laden.

The principles I want to zero in on now are those that allow us to capture the mind of our enemies or opponents—surprise and speed. The SEALs have gotten so good at acting with speed that they almost always surprise their enemies. The SEALs who captured Bin Laden were into the compound so quickly no one had time to respond . . . they were out of there before the Pakistan military even woke up. Their high-level tactics for shifting gears midstream enabled them to execute a perfect mission despite one of two helicopters crashing to the ground! That is an excellent example of how agility allows you to maintain velocity for extraordinary results.

In business, speed—or velocity—keeps you ahead of the competition and keeps them off balance, surprising them at every turn. Apple gets kudos for their creativity, but Samsung gets the award for speed—they stunned the iPad creator with how quickly they produced a competing tablet. Google will get kudos for inventing Google Glasses but it will be interesting to see who gets the award for speed in copying this innovative product and claiming the market. Let's face it—we've become so interconnected through instantaneous information transfers that whole segments of the global population can shift directions almost immediately.

You are well aware that the pace of change is accelerating as technology pushes the reaches of globalization. Remain static and you lose momentum, visibility, and opportunities. Eventually you become stuck in a cryogenic deep freeze as the world blazes by. SEALs have learned to plan and execute with blinding speed, in military time. Traditionally it takes a ground unit about three days to plan and achieve a target, but the SEALs can plan and then hit multiple targets in rapid succession in mere hours, even when obstacles arise. Like the SEALs, WOS leaders set the conditions for rapid execution by:

- trusting those in the field
- applying standard operating procedures
- utilizing a shoot, move, and communicate process

Trust Those in the Field

Trust is the currency of leadership. It must flow both ways: Soldiers must trust their leaders, and leaders must trust their soldiers. Low trust leads to more costly and slower execution because it reduces risk-taking and innovation—it essentially kills your ability to remain agile, thus gumming up the works. High trust leads to the opposite.

Of course, trust is easier to develop when the players executing a mission are face to face; things get tricky when they've never met or are mainly working from disparate locations. This is becoming an increasing problem for modern companies. For example, the Internet company Yahoo! was an early adopter of the dispersed virtual workforce, thought to be the way of the future. When new CEO Marissa Mayer came onboard years later, she reportedly noted that the productivity of many remote workers had dropped off, and she faced an uphill battle trying to change the company's culture (which had lost its cohesion and emphasis on collaboration) with much of the workforce remaining at home. To the howls of many staffers, Yahoo! eliminated the work-from-home option in early 2013 and told those workers who couldn't or wouldn't come into the office to quit. This scenario is a serious consideration for businesses as the push for flexible work arrangements continues. Teams must be tethered closely to perform at an elite level. Imagine a SEAL Team working remotely by e-mail and conference calls, and then showing up to nail Bin Laden at the prescribed hour.

Does this mean employees can't work remotely? Like it or not, there is just no substitute for looking another human in the eye and establishing a "soul level" contact. Further, it's difficult to build deep trust with someone who isn't "on the job." If it's simply not possible to have everyone work onsite, you can establish more trust with the following tips:

- Use videoconferencing when possible. Skype is a simple tool I use often.
- Do the important planning meetings in person. If someone can't be there, then conference them in.
- Have weekly briefs to synchronize efforts, in person or through conference calls.
- Have postevent celebrations and encourage live attendance.
- Look for any opportunity to facilitate a meet-up between team members.

When I launched the nationwide mentor program for SEAL candidates, I made it a priority to visit each one of the twenty-six recruiting offices around the country. I could have stayed put behind my desk and the comfortable mirage of getting things done via e-mail. In fact, I was not contractually required to spend any time at the recruiting districts, let alone two weeks a month on the road at my own expense. But guess what? Each commanding officer and recruiting team was thrilled about the visits, many questions and concerns surfaced that would not have otherwise, and the program was a huge success.

Planners in the rear, both business leaders and SEAL officers, have the luxury of time and safety to guide their decision-making, but their disconnection from ground-level truth often makes it hard for them to trust information from the field and see the best course of action. On one hand, they have the benefit of advisors and a strategic-level view, which means decisions will be thoroughly considered. On the other hand, those decisions may not be supported by field-level input, be timely, or make sense to the operator experiencing the immediacy of the situation.

I have seen more bad decisions made by the rear echelon than good ones due to lack of trust; therefore, I believe it's important to trust the opinions and decisions of those in the field and closest to the action. When leaders micromanage from the rear, as so many do, it reduces trust between all parties to a decision and leaves field officers reluctant to make the call, even if they're certain about it, for fear of being second-guessed or reprimanded. This leads to a downward spiral of performance and costly errors of judgment. Conversely, leaders who macromanage from the rear allow their field teams to make decisions appropriate for the field level, while you in the rear can make decisions appropriate for your level, such as how to support and align missions, deal with contingencies, and provide top-cover in the form of supporting assets and accepting accountability if the field unit screws up. Trusting the decisions of those in the field allows them to operate with more speed and agility, decreasing costs and enhancing results. Ensure they know the plan, trust them to do their job, and then get out of their way.

Apply Standard Operating Procedures

Standard operating procedures (SOPs) are simplified routines (actually processes) for common tasks that free up the minds of your field operators, allowing them to perform the tasks almost on autopilot while they focus their valuable resources on responding to the small percentage of problems that are new and unique. Certain aspects of a mission are the same for every mission. For the SEALs these would include such aspects as the mission planning and briefing process, the way the men organize themselves for each specific, routine task (i.e., patrolling an area, riding in the helicopter, or entering a structure during a direct action), and communication protocols. We train these procedures until every SEAL can perform them the same way and with precision every time. This allows the operators to spend valuable time and energy planning the more nuanced aspects of a mission and rapidly responding to changes in the environment.

Let's look at a product launch. The basics, such as project management, copyrighting or trademarking, creating websites, and search engine optimization follow the same steps every time. This is why it is always easier the second and third time you do the same mission, assuming the organization learns and doesn't have to reinvent the wheel. These aspects are practical routines without which a product launch cannot occur (at least, not effectively) and can thus make great SOPs. You can likewise anticipate certain kinds of problems that frequently occur, such as a server going down or a manufacturing delay, and thus you can outline contingency plans for these one-off challenges in advance. However, with every new product you launch, you must independently plan and execute the nuances of its sales campaign—every product will make a different promise to a different target market. If your team already knows the common steps by heart, they can devote all their time and creativity to highlighting what makes a product unique and exploring innovative ways to reach its ideal customers. And if something unexpected changes, such as the release of new research that affects public perception of your product, you can easily shift fire to address that problem without worrying about keeping the ball rolling for the overall mission.

Some areas around which you can develop SOPs include:

- your battle rhythm—daily, weekly, monthly, quarterly, and annual planning
- opportunity analysis using KISS methods
- communication protocols, especially for e-mail, meetings, debriefs, and media inquiries
- contingency plans for natural disasters and chance incidences like a shooting or kidnapping

Creating SOPs begins with an analysis of the critical nodes of a process. Critical nodes are the parts of your processes that, if interrupted, would cause a cascading failure of the entire system. You want to create SOPs around protecting critical nodes and addressing failures if they occur despite your best efforts, but you also want to put some resources into shoring up those systems that absolutely must be working for the overall effort to succeed so they won't devolve into distractions later. As with most concepts, you can work on this individually, at the team level, and in your organization. Consider: What systems or activities, if they failed, would bring your entire mission to a halt? What systems or activities would directly affect your ability to remain agile and to maintain velocity?

My SEAL Team THREE commanding officer, Commander McRaven, performed a critical node analysis of the Team when he took over command in 1994. He noted how our infrastructure and policies positioned us best to fight a war in Southeast Asia, a throwback to the Vietnam days. Additionally, we lacked language skills necessary for developing an agility and cultural sensitivity to the region he saw as America's next battleground—the Middle East. Understanding how our weakness at these critical nodes could significantly slow the team's ability to respond to new threats appearing anywhere besides Southeast Asia and even sabotage our efforts once we deployed, he formulated a preemptive plan. McRaven repositioned ST-3 structures to better focus on the Middle East and sent the SEALs to language school for Arabic and Farsi. His reinforcement of our critical nodes combined with a front-sight focus on his mission as commanding officer—to train and deploy us for maritime special operations—prepared us for the next war on our horizon, as opposed to the last one. When Al Qaeda attacked in 2001, ST-3 responded quickly and nimbly, thanks to McRaven's efforts.

Once you've identified your critical nodes, break them down into routine and nonroutine tasks required to maintain their role in the overall process of operating your business and for pursuing specific, commonly repeated missions. You should also consider what one-offs you must perform to reinforce your critical nodes in general, which will enable you to remain front-sight focused on every mission with which you engage. Finally, create SOPs (typically a numbered list or flow chart mapping out who takes what actions) around the routine tasks, and train them until the team can do them in their sleep. As mentioned earlier, this allows the team to now focus valuable planning and execution time and energy on the important and nonroutine tasks of the mission.

Every team member responsible for performing a given task must master the SOP. For more complicated or crucial SOPs, such as those around critical nodes, you will want to ensure at least two team members master each SOP for redundancy, in much the same way that a pilot and copilot both master the SOP checklists for flying a Boeing 747. Similarly, you will want to prepare yourself with contingencies, which can and should become documented SOPs as well, for when things go awry. No plan survives contact with the enemy!

SOPs aren't created or trained overnight. However, once you're using them effectively, this simple documentation and rehearsal process, when applied consistently, will allow you to plan and execute with the lightning fast acuity exemplary of an offensive mind-set.

Shoot, Move, and Communicate

Agility and velocity are crucial for leaders as our business climate increasingly takes on the attributes of a battlefield, and are essential components of an offensive mind-set. SEAL leaders remain agile by maintaining situational awareness, developing and applying solid SOPs, building redundancy and contingencies into their plan, and mastering the ability to "shift fire" on a moment's notice—to try new things without fear of failure and to fail forward fast. That agility enables the leader to maintain velocity during a mission. In the thick of things, one tool SEALS use to heighten agility and maintain velocity is a "shoot, move, and communicate" process called the OODA loop. "Shoot, move, and communicate" references a military tactical decision-making concept that boils down to the acronym OODA. Coined by the late Air Force Colonel John Boyd, this simple and elegant tool can similarly help business leaders maintain agility and velocity in their tactical business decisions.

The acronym, which stands for "Observe, Orient, Decide, and Act," was developed to clarify the rapid-fire life and death decisions made during aerial combat. This process is precisely what we need for rapid execution in business. The OODA loop is a mental model that compels you to process and respond to information quickly. In doing so, you get very good at making good decisions on the fly. You will avoid analyzing things to death, or getting caught in watered down solutions that tend to result from group process decisions.

Boyd's simple but powerful observation was that if you can speed up your own decision-making cycle while slowing down your opponent's, the outcome will veer in your favor. You speed up your cycle with good SOPs, effective macromanagement, and aggressive decision-making. You would slow your enemies' (your competitors') cycle by capturing their minds with speed and surprise, forcing them to react and keeping them on the defensive. Whoever navigates their OODA loop the fastest will have the upper hand.

When my friend Alden launched the Perfect Pushup, the other fitness companies with pushup handles didn't even see him coming. Alden observed his situation and saw that his initial product had failed. He oriented his thinking and dwindling resources to create a new, simpler-to-use product—the Perfect Pushup. Then he decided on a direct response marketing strategy that bypassed his competitors' normal marketing channels, the action taking them in a surprise move that allowed no time to respond. While his competitors remained committed to a traditional distribution model for their exercise equipment—selling through big-box retailers such as Walmart, Target, and Sports Authority—Alden went directly to the customer through targeted ads in men's magazines and an infomercial campaign. He quickly gained the upper hand in capturing the attention of consumers and kept the pressure on with new ads and deeper market penetration with new infomercials, reinvesting all his early profits back into the marketing engine. Only after he had thoroughly defined the Perfect Pushup in the consumers' minds did he place the product in stores alongside his competitors' products. He continued the OODA loop process, getting his decision cycle tighter and faster, while his competitors fell behind with their slower response cycle.

The offensive leader does not kill things with overplanning—rather, when the landscape shifts, as it always does, you will shift with it using the OODA loop, which I'll teach you to apply in the Exercises section.

Thinking offense, all the time, aligns your mind and spirit in a forward-momentum, active effort that will allow you to tackle anything with unwavering confidence in your ability to win. While your competition puts their energy into protecting themselves or hedging their bets against potential downturns, you'll focus your intensity and dive forward, scanning for change and adjusting rapidly as you learn for uncommonly effective execution. Supported by a keen awareness, you'll move so fast and so smoothly your enemies won't even see you coming—nor will they see you as you blow right past them to nab opportunities. Why? Because you follow the Way of the SEAL, the edge that helps you achieve success in every situation.

★ ★ ★ EXERCISES ★ ★ ★

YELLOW RADAR

Use this exercise to practice maintaining a "yellow state" of passive alertness. For example, when going to a restaurant, ensure that your yellow radar is switched "on." Scan the environment outside the restaurant and see what you notice. Try to note how many people are there, what they are wearing, and look for patterns. Then scan for anything that does not fit the pattern. For example, is there anyone waiting to eat alone? Is there someone standing around who doesn't look like he or she is engaged in going somewhere or doing something? Without being paranoid, just notice if there is anything unusual and use your gut to feel the surroundings.

When you enter the restaurant, scan the inside just as you did the outside. Note patterns and anything that doesn't fit. Ask the host for a seat near the back of the restaurant, where you can casually observe while you are enjoying your meal. Keep a mental log of the activities during the time at the restaurant. Maintain your passive-alert "yellow" state of awareness throughout your time there. Repeat this drill when you go to the movies, shopping, to the bank, and so on, and eventually it will become a permanent state of elevated awareness that will serve you well at home, at work, when traveling, and even while playing.

DEVELOP YOUR STANDARD OPERATING PROCEDURES

When thinking offensively, you're preparing for the future and focusing on your ability to act quickly and smoothly in the moment. To identify what aspects of your business you can turn into standard operating procedures, ask the following questions:

- What processes or activities do I or my team perform repeatedly?

- What are the critical nodes of those processes?

- What core tasks related to these critical nodes are repeatable, measurable, and trainable?

Now write your SOPs down step by step and develop a simple training plan around them for your operators. For maximum success, use the crawl, walk, run model: Seek accuracy in the task one time initially, followed by accuracy at a moderate pace, and then finally aim for accurate execution with velocity. Don't forget to build in redundancy in case of unexpected problems—remember, the world is chaotic, and destiny favors the prepared.

OODA LOOP

The OODA loop is a rapid planning tool—recall its original intention for air-to-air combat. For business leaders, the tool is best used when you are pressured to make quick decisions in a fluid environment, such as the scenario described previously with my friend Alden's Perfect Pushup.

Observe your position relative to the competition. How is their next move going to affect you? Use your situational awareness skills to look at the details as well as the big picture. For example, your product is first to market and superior in quality, yet on the pricey side of the market range. You observe your competition introduce a lower-priced knockoff, and you expect them to overtake you.

Orient to the new reality you've observed as fast as possible without making a move (yet). What is your goal—for example, to beat out the competition and regain market share at any cost, or to maintain quality, which may mean exploring new markets that appreciate value and are less price sensitive, abandoning the product line to explore a new one, or finding new ways to educate your customers about the value? What effect will lowering your price have on your margins? How will your competition respond—will they start a price war, and what will that mean for your company? Orientation is processing and analyzing the gathered intelligence quickly relative to your normal planning cycle. In a SEAL op, the OODA loop is almost real time. For a company, it may mean collapsing your planning cycles from months to days or weeks.

Decide on an action. This is where the rubber meets the road. Acting on a good decision is better than not acting on a great decision. So make a good decision, one that speeds up your OODA loop, while offering the potential to slow down the other players in your cat-and-mouse game. In our example, you decide to back your product with an information campaign emphasizing the superior quality and prestige of ownership to differentiate it in the market. Simultaneously you file for intellectual property protection and enlist the support of your loyal customers to blog about how amazing your product is and to be wary of the knockoffs.

Act and instantly seek feedback. Monitor the thought-leader blogs in your space and watch for any reaction from your competition. Learn from any feedback, reset your observation post, and continue cycling through the loop.

TRAINING IN THE WAY OF THE SEAL

You may never know what results come from your actions.
But if you take no action, there will be no results.
—Mohandas Gandhi, Indian Civil Rights activist
and leader (1869–1948)

I believe strongly that, after a certain age, if we aren't seeking growth in life, we will start moving backward. This is certainly true about our physical bodies—if left to nature, the human body develops, grows, and evolves, performs at its peak for a period, then starts to degenerate and weaken, slowly at first and more quickly later. However, we can stimulate our bodies to continue growth relative to each phase of life with the right nutrition and activities. Same with our mental capacity, which to a certain extent is fully developed by our mid-twenties. But what happens after that? Do we then strive for constant improvement or settle into the belief that we are who we are and leave it at that?

Clearly, we can develop our mental capacities beyond where we settle in early adulthood. The point of this book is to show you how. As you activate your training, you will integrate the principles into your life at a deep level until they become part of you, shaping your reality now and in the future. The tools will serve you along the way, often in new and surprising ways as you develop the clarity, focus, and power to get extraordinary results.

Before we start, let me warn you: There is no such thing as perfection. We are all flawed in some marvelous ways. However, there is such a thing as a perfect effort. Through perfect effort, you will see success with the training even though you may experience a temporary setback or failure (remember, every failure is an opportunity to learn and grow). Day by day, in every way, you will get better and better. Even if it is by 1 percent every day, over time that will lead to uncommon results. You will train and practice daily in a manner that is right for you now. As time goes on your training plan will shift to accommodate your evolving needs and the growth you experience as a result of the work. Let's look at the principles of training in more detail, before we get into creating the plan itself.

Slow Is Smooth, Smooth Is Fast

Never give up on a dream just because of the time it will take to accomplish it. The time will pass anyway.
—EARL NIGHTINGALE, AMERICAN MOTIVATIONAL
SPEAKER AND AUTHOR (1921-1989)

When I first started with this type of integral training, I thought I could accelerate my development just by working harder. I tried to force-feed myself Zen meditation, karate classes, dozens of books, seminars, and more physical training than I'd already been doing. More would get me there faster, I assumed. Wrong. This approach led to frustration and burnout, and a break from the training. Turns out you can't force your own development; you can only facilitate it.

Understanding this now, I encourage you to take a "slow is smooth" approach. When we slow things down and seek perfect effort, our body and mind absorb the concepts and techniques more completely. This ensures they are available for us in "smooth and fast" form when we need to act.

In the SEALS, we used a similar concept, approaching each training period with a "crawl, walk, run" rhythm. Like a child, you must crawl before you walk and walk before you run. The crawl stage of training is where you learn the fundamental theory and basic skills—that's what this book has provided you with so far. Training the fundamentals will allow you to build a foundation to move faster and go deeper into the training. Without the foundation, you could veer off track and get unbalanced, or fall off altogether out of frustration. This stage can take as long as you need and will depend upon your level of skill and time restraints when you start—some of my students spend just a few weeks getting up to speed on the basics while others take up to a year. Embrace your process and enjoy learning the new skills.

Typically, after a month or two of regular training, you will want to step things up. Welcome to the "walk" stage, where you are now comfortable with the practices, are seeing progress, but haven't yet fully integrated and habituated the training. You start to develop physical and mental control and emotional resilience to life's challenges. You feel the lightness of a simplified life and see the results of front-sight focus applied to your missions. You begin to show up as different—uncommonly confident and successful—to others. But the walk phase is fraught with challenge: Some end their training at this point, typically sliding back to their old ways after all the excitement and newness has worn off. I've offered some recommendations in this chapter to help you stay the course.

The final (or "run") stage of development is about performing at your peak in a flow of unconscious competence. Remember, mastery in the Way of the SEAL is not about working hard until you arrive at some mystical destination where you get knighted and sit at the round table. The reason I call it "the Way" is because it points the way for your journey and provides a strategy, tactics, tools, and motivation. In the Way of the SEAL, we are striving to navigate that journey with increasing awareness and power. Once you set foot onto this path, you begin to find extraordinary results through doing ordinary things extraordinarily well—and it eventually comes naturally. That is mastery.

The Way of the SEAL Integral Development Model

The unexamined life is not worth living.
—SOCRATES, GREEK PHILOSOPHER (469 BCE–399 BCE)

The Way of the SEAL asks you to build on and acquire a variety of skills that will enable you to think and act like an elite warrior to achieve extraordinary results in your life. In order to help you learn and master these skills, this book introduces you to a number of drills, exercises, and tools. For example, Still Water Runs Deep is a technique or drill to help you create sacred silence, which in turn cultivates the skill of mindfulness or awareness. FITS, PROP, and SMACC are mission-planning tools that support front-sight focus. Throughout, I also discuss several practices without offering direct instruction because I assume that you already know what they are or will seek out a more detailed guide to those you choose to pursue. Yoga, for instance, is a practice I encourage my students to pursue as part of their training because it encompasses all five mountains and reinforces many skills involving mindfulness and awareness including physiological control, attention control, flexibility, core strength, and more.

As you probably understand by now, some of these activities are meant for use as needed, while others are most effective if performed regularly, whether for a few minutes or a bit longer. One of the most effective ways to start translating all this information into an integral training plan is to use a morning and evening ritual, the basic outline for which you will find in Appendix 2. Even if yours must be very short, at a bare minimum I recommend you start with these training components, which combine a number of the key drills and exercises into a daily sequence that will help you focus your efforts while starting and ending your days with a potent training session. I find that the morning and evening rituals are an indispensable component for my students because they ensure that you are strengthening in the mental, emotional, intuitional, and spiritual mountains with critical, foundational techniques each day. The morning ritual is particularly effective in its ability to set the tone for a positive, energized day during which you are more likely to use spot practices and implement your new skills to greater effect. The evening ritual provides the perfect complement, helping you lock in the achievements of your day, glean the most important lessons or insights, and go to bed with a feeling of satisfaction and confidence in what the future holds.

In Appendix 2 I've also given you outlines for two more rituals: the pre-event and postevent rituals. Done as needed, such as before or after a competition or business meeting, these sequences ensure that you set the stage for optimal performance and then offer you healthy closure by helping you identify where you excelled and where there's room for improvement; find the silver lining of any setbacks or failures; learn from your experience; reset your training plan to reflect your new insights, and finally return your focus to the present.

In addition to the rituals, depending on your level of experience with personal development, your time restrictions, and your particular needs, you will incorporate any number of other drills, exercises, and practices for an integral training plan that will propel you along on the Way of the SEAL. To refresh your memory, integral training means that you will cross-train the five human capacities or "five mountains" I discussed briefly in the introduction to this book. They are:

1. **Physical:** for developing functional fitness and bodily control

2. **Mental:** for developing focus and mental toughness

3. **Emotional:** for developing emotional control and resilience

4. **Intuitional:** for developing awareness and intuition

5. **Spiritual:** for developing your spirit or kokoro, the merging of your heart and mind in action

These capacities span the eight WOS principles and are so intertwined that it's difficult to train them in isolation; rather you will cross-train to develop the five mountains together, which in turn will support your efforts to master the WOS principles. In this book, I've primarily focused on the mental, emotional, and intuitional mountains, with acknowledgement of how training in these capacities naturally strengthens and deepens your warrior spirit. I haven't devoted much time to the physical mountain. Yet you'll notice in this chapter that the training plans all include physical activity as a necessary component.

The reason I include physical activity in WOS training is the same reason I teach my SEALFIT students physical training first: It's easiest to see and feel progress, or lack thereof, with physical training. I want them (and you) to break through physical barriers and limitations, which forges a channel to the other four mountains in the process. Additionally, physical training helps you develop control over your body, and makes it a stable, healthy, and powerful platform for your entire life.

In putting together your physical training plan, I urge you to focus on functional fitness—that is, a program that develops strength, stamina, endurance, work capacity, and durability. Functional fitness trains you to handle any kind of real-world physical task, whether that includes a 20-mile trek to a remote mountaintop or just lugging bags home from the grocery store. I also recommend supplementing functional fitness with a somatic, mind-body practice such as yoga or tai chi, which can improve your flexibility and muscle strength as well as your concentration, stillness, and self-awareness. (These practices, however, will not take care of all the physical needs of your body as it moves on a daily basis, and are not substitutes for physical training.)

Assess Your Starting Point

Ability is what you are capable of, motivation determines what
you do,and attitude determines how well you do it.
—LOU HOLTZ, AMERICAN SPORTSWRITER
AND RETIRED FOOTBALL COACH (1939–)

I've said it before, but it bears repeating: If you desire serious change in your life, you can't get there by focusing on what you don't want. Experiencing failure, even visualized or imagined failure, in advance only produces anxiety to further weigh you down. Rather, you have learned in this book how to experience success in advance by visualizing victory and directing positive mental and physical energy toward achieving it. However, in order to get to that victory, you need to know where you are starting from.

In this section, we will work through a self-assessment to help you select the right tools and training for you. As you contemplate the questions, you'll get a sense of whether or not you need more development in a certain mountain. Once you've completed this process, make a list of any WOS principles that struck you as particularly important for where you are in your life right now—as you read through this book, one or more principles probably resonated for you immediately and deeply. Finally, make a list of every extracurricular activity you're doing right now. For instance, perhaps you regularly attend a yoga class once or twice a week, or perhaps you've been a CrossFit enthusiast for years. Maybe you already practice visualization and use positive mantras.

Your findings in the assessment may prompt you to replace or scale back some practices in favor of others, but you may also find that you're currently satisfying certain requirements. If you are already a martial artist, you may not want to add yoga to your routine; if you're already functionally fit, you won't need to add more physical training to your plan (and you may even choose to reallocate some of your workout time to other needs). The time you spend visualizing may be structured more effectively.

Once you've got a clear picture of your starting point, we'll move on to choosing tools and practices as well as a "battle rhythm" for your customized training plan.

Self-Assessment Questions

Physical

1. Do I follow a thorough functional training regimen at the gym, rather than just using the elliptical and a few weight machines or running a few miles in my neighborhood?

2. Am I comfortable and stable in my body throughout the day and during physical activity?

3. Am I able to sit still for long periods without physical discomfort?

4. Do I meet my doctor's criteria for good health at my age?

5. Am I conscious of what I eat and drink throughout the day, rather than grabbing whatever is immediately handy or what satisfies my craving?

6. Am I generally free of injury, illness, and general malaise, able to meet my commitments and attend work and social activities without problem?

If you answered "no" or "maybe" (which really means "I don't know") to more than three of these questions, you would benefit from a solid functional physical training program. I encourage you to begin a routine such as SEALFIT, CrossFit, or P90X for one hour, three times a week. A "maybe" answer to a few of these questions will require you to investigate an improvement to your current routine (same recommendations apply). A "yes" answer to most of these questions means that you are doing well—good job on this front; no need to make changes to your program.

Mental

1. Do I regularly train to cultivate my mental strength as if it were the same as conditioning my body?

2. Do I respond to stressful situations like an airplane pilot calmly following an emergency procedure checklist, exercising control over my response?

3. Am I able to bypass "analysis paralysis" by swiftly making decisions in which I feel confident and then taking action?

4. Can I easily distinguish between facts and interpretation in any given situation?

5. Do I habitually persevere when faced with a challenge, rarely giving up?

If you answered "no" or "maybe" to three or more of these questions, then you will want to emphasize mental development in your training plan. The tools to start with are Box Breathing and Still Water Runs Deep, then developing your DIRECT process with a daily commitment to a concentration practice, eliminating negative input and developing a positively charged mantra. If you answered "yes," then you will emphasize other aspects of the training while continuing what you are doing now for mental development. I also recommend Box Breathing and all aspects of the DIRECT process.

Emotional

1. Am I able to keep my negative emotional reactions from resulting in decisions, actions, or statements that I later regret?

2. Do I allow myself to feel and then express my emotions in a healthy, productive manner?

3. In a moment of strong emotion, am I able to reflect on negative feelings to see what's triggering me? Do I know what triggers emotional responses in myself most frequently?

4. When faced with a stressful situation, such as a road rage encounter or an issue at the airlines counter, am I able to modify my emotional state at will?

5. Can I think of a time when I felt anger but decided to just let it go, thus creating peace for everyone involved (and not out of fear of confrontation)?

6. Is it easy for me to be intimate and open in relationships?

If you answered "no" or "maybe" to three or more of these questions then your emotional development will require a focus of effort as well. The primary tools to work with are authentic communication, emotional awareness and the BOO visualization exercise. Yoga is a good long-term aid in this area, as are the 20X challenges you'll set for yourself. If you are a solid "yes" in this area, then you can move on to intuition and spirit.

Intuitional

1. In my last few conversations, did I listen more than speak?

2. Can I describe the clothing and appearance of three strangers I saw this morning?

3. Do I find myself slow to pass judgment, thereby avoiding sticky situations or jumping to conclusions?

4. Do I generally feel at peace with myself, regularly experiencing moments of high self-esteem and satisfaction?

5. Can I think of three times in the past week that I actively and authentically listened to someone else?

6. Do I acknowledge and reinforce intuitive flashes or insights or do I brush them off as random and unimportant?

If you answered "no" or "maybe" to three or more of these questions, then your intuition is lying dormant. Time to wake it up! The primary tools for you are Still Water Runs Deep, the mind gym, Box Breathing, and yoga or another somatic practice.

Spiritual

1. In a moment of crisis or indecision, do I have a clear stand with articulated values to keep my feet in the sand?

2. Do I know my purpose, and am I directing most of my time and energy toward fulfilling it?

3. Am I able to see the "big picture" and suffer challenges or setbacks with a smile and a positive attitude?

4. Am I willing and able to make sacrifices in order to achieve my goals and dreams?

5. Do I feel that my life is filled with value?

6. Do I generally feel present and peaceful?

If you found yourself answering "no" to two or three questions in this category, you will want to revisit components related to Principles 1 and 2, especially devoting more time to your WOS Assessment and completing the Focus Plan worksheets in Appendix 1. I recommend that you review your daily and weekly Focus Plans twice a day (make it part of your morning and evening rituals). Then, spend at least twenty minutes once per week reviewing your monthly Focus Plan so you can ensure the following week's Focus Plan is still properly moving you toward your goals. Likewise, once a month, spend at least twenty minutes reviewing your quarterly and/or annual Focus Plan so you can align and create the next month's Focus Plan. Additionally, I strongly encourage you to cultivate a religious or spiritual practice of your own choosing—if the tradition your parents raised you in doesn't feel authentic, make the hard choice and find another one. Whether it's a Christian church service, prayer to a Hindu god, or an atheist-friendly meditation, weakness in this mountain is best addressed by incorporating a regular practice that brings you peace and gives you a sense that there is some deeper meaning or higher order in life.

When You're Strapped for Time

I understand how difficult it can be to find more time in your already hectic life. Though on the surface it may seem like you need to leave your job and focus on training full time with WOS, that's just an illusion. The reality is that the tools and practices are easy to learn and weave into your life. Furthermore, the longer you train, the more focused, simplified, and clear your life will get, thereby further freeing up valuable training time.

The Bureau of Labor Statistics reported that in 2012, the average American aged fifteen or older spent 2.8 hours per day watching TV. That's almost twenty hours a week! Imagine all the things you could do to positively impact your mind, body, and spirit with that much leisure time. I know it isn't easy, but unless your livelihood requires you to remain tuned in to current events on an up-to-the-minute basis, I encourage you to eliminate TV. If that's just not possible for you, then at minimum eliminate any viewing of television news for at least thirty days as you begin your training. After this time, only watch it if something important is going on that requires your attention (like a natural disaster).

Why avoid TV news? The thing is, most people are addicted to a constant flood of what is passed off as news but is mostly just superfluous nonsense about celebrities, politicians, and minor events. Additionally, because of the "scare factor" necessary for keeping eyes glued to the screen (which in turn attracts advertisers and income),

TV news is notoriously negative and will have a big impact on your subconscious over time—as with any high-functioning computer, the output of your mind is shaped by what you put into it.

To save valuable time, stay "in the know" with the real information you need, and avoid negative input, scan newspaper and online news headlines instead. Then you can dig deep into the article itself if the information seems critical. I like to scan Google news headlines twice a day and the *Wall Street Journal* whenever I can, looking for headlines that affect my life, or that are indicative of business trends or growing threats that might affect me personally or professionally.

Here are a few more tips for those of you who truly feel like you can't wring one free minute out of your day:

- Spend a little less time in the shower or reading the morning paper or get up just a half-hour earlier to make time for your morning ritual, which can be as short as twenty minutes. Include yoga or another mindful movement routine (five minutes), Box Breathing (five minutes), and a Still Water Runs Deep visualization (five minutes). Wrap up with a quick review of your focus plan for the day and perhaps a brief visualization of your perfect day unfolding (five minutes).

- During the day, periodically pause to apply the "What Dog Are You Feeding?" exercise and recite your power mantra, especially effective when you feel negative or as if you're losing focus or control over your day. You can also do these when you have as little as five minutes of break time, like when you're grabbing a coffee or waiting for the elevator.

- Instead of going out to lunch, use your lunch hour for physical training—you can complete a good functional fitness routine in less than an hour. Eat at your desk later or implement an "as needed" fueling program, eating small nutritious snacks throughout the day only when you feel hungry.

- Take a ten-minute power break in the midafternoon to recharge your batteries, and make sure you wrap up your workday with strong intent. Try Box Breathing (five minutes) and a brief "Future Me" visualization (five minutes).

- During dinner, turn off your phones and TVs and practice authentic communication with your loved ones.

- In the evening, instead of watching television or surfing the Internet, read a book—even just fifteen minutes of reading a great novel or an inspiring nonfiction book can take you to another world and leave you a better person. This is a fun way to increase your concentration and enhance your optimism and positive attitude by taking your focus off yourself.

- Before bed, perform your twenty-minute evening ritual, which should include: Box Breathing (five minutes), What's the Silver Lining? (five minutes), writing your focus plan for tomorrow (five minutes), and visualizing your next day flowing effortlessly as you achieve your goals (five minutes).

Everyone can find a way to squeeze in some training. It may mean changing your sleep or work schedule a bit. (However, it's important not to sacrifice a good night's sleep—if you get up earlier for more quiet time, be sure you go to bed earlier, too). It may mean simplifying your life by letting go of some obligations or delegating tasks to others. For most, it's a matter of replacing inefficient time with efficient time. However you do it, in whatever small increments with which you must start, WOS training will change your life, providing the calmness and focus to achieve your goals while enabling you to give yourself and your family the love and support you all deserve.

Your Way of the SEAL Training Plan

Twenty years from now you will be more disappointed by the things that you didn't do than by the ones you did do. So throw off the bowlines. Sail away from the safe harbor. Catch the trade winds in your sails. Explore. Dream. Discover.

—Mark Twain, American author and humorist (1835–1910)

Now that you have a clear picture of what you're already doing and what you need, check out the Training Tools At a Glance below. You'll note that every drill, exercise, or practice listed is marked to show its role in developing each mountain and WOS principle. I also suggest how much time to devote to each. Browse the list and use your self-assessment to guide you in selecting the right tools and practices for you in the development of your WOS training plan. In general, if the suggested frequency offers a range, choose the amount of training time

Training Tools At a Glance

Drill/Exercise/ Ritual	WOS Principle/Skill	Time Requirement	Physical
WOS Assessment*	Establish Your Set Point	Check in monthly for needed updates/changes	
"Envision Your Future Me"*	Establish Your Set Point	5–15 minutes daily	
Still Water Runs Deep*	Develop Front-Sight Focus	5–15 minutes daily	
Fantasizing with Purpose (aka "practice visualization")	Develop Front-Sight Focus	5–15 minutes daily	
The Sentinel at the Gate*	Develop Front-Sight Focus	1 minute several times a day	
DIRECT Your Mind*	Develop Front-Sight Focus	1 minute several times a day	
KISS*	Develop Front-Sight Focus	5–15 minutes monthly	
The Idea Lab	Bulletproof Your Mission	5–15 minutes as needed	
Transmuting Pain into Positivity	Do Today What Others Won't	5 minutes as needed	x

based on your experience with that activity and with your needs. For example, if you're an experienced visualizer, you may only choose to incorporate a brief "Future Me" visualization into your day, whereas someone new to the concept of envisioning should probably devote fifteen minutes or more daily to strengthen that muscle and their mental toughness.

The bulk of your training plan will be daily tasks planned in a weekly format. That's what you will see in the three sample plans that follow. There are a few additional weekly, monthly, quarterly, and annual components, which I will note with each plan as well. The daily tasks in my plan take me three to four hours to complete (most of that is my physical training, which is key for my lifestyle and career and accordingly commands the lion's share of my daily training time). If you have less time to devote to your training, your plan must adjust accordingly—with slightly less focus on physical training, you could still accomplish everything in an hour or two. I will say, however, that I'm amazed at how much time I save in my life in the long run having improved myself in all five mountains, which allows me to think and act more effectively on a daily basis and in all situations. My physical health also has cut down on time spent in illness, doctor visits, and recovery.

Mental	Emotional	Intuition	Spirit	Page
x	x		x	22
x		x	x	27
x	x	x	x	38
x				43
x	x	x		52
x	x	x		53
x	x		x	55
x		x		71
x	x			83

Training Tools At a Glance (continued)

Drill/Exercise/ Ritual	WOS Principle/Skill	Time Requirement	Physical
Bring It!	Do Today What Others Won't	Weekly or monthly	x
Find Your 20X Factor*	Do Today What Others Won't	Quarterly or annually	x
Transform Your Emotions*	Forge Mental Toughness	As needed	
Box Breathing*	Forge Mental Toughness	5–15 minutes daily	x
Turning Stress into Success*	Forge Mental Toughness	5–15 minutes as needed	x
What Dog Are You Feeding?*	Forge Mental Toughness	1 minutes several times a day	x
Setting SMART Goals*	Forge Mental Toughness	Check in daily and review / update monthly, quarterly and annually	
Making Decisiveness a Habit	Break Things	As needed	
Making Variety a Habit	Break Things	As needed	
Finding the Silver Lining*	Break Things	1-2 minutes daily or as needed	
Identifying Opportunities	Break Things	10-20 minutes quarterly	
The KIM Game	Build Your Intuition	5-15 minutes weekly	
Hone Your Senses	Build Your Intuition	5-15 minutes weekly	
Awaken Your Intuition*	Build Your Intuition	5-15 minutes as needed	
Authentic Communication*	Build Your Intuition	10-30 minutes daily	
Change Your Words, Change Your Attitude*	Think Offense	As needed	
Yellow Radar*	Think Offense, All the Time	Periodically	
SEALFIT, CrossFit, or similar*	functional fitness	60 minutes/ 3-5 x times a week	x
Sacred Silence (Still Water Runs Deep or other meditation)*	mindfulness/awareness	5-15 minutes as needed	
Somatic Practice (yoga, chi gong, tai chi, dance)*	mindfulness/awareness	5-15 minutes daily and up to 60 minutes 2-3 times a week	x
Positive Self-Talk & Mantra*	positive self-talk/attention control	As needed	
Focus Planning & Goal Review*		5-15 minutes daily	
Professional Therapy*		60 minutes as needed (minimum annually)	

Mental	Emotional	Intuition	Spirit	Page
x	x			90
x	x		x	90
	x			100
x		x	x	108
x				109
x	x			109
x				110
x	x			128
x	x			131
x	x			132
x				133
x				139
		x		143
		x		150
x	x	x	x	155
x	x	x		159
x	x	x		183
x				
x	x	x	x	
x	x	x	x	
x	x		x	
x				
x	x	x	x	

Notes on Training Tools At a Glance:

---

1. Foundational elements are marked with an asterisk. These are key components for all WOS leaders, regardless of where you are with your training, though your experience and needs may dictate how often you incorporate them.

2. Time requirements indicate a suggested range along which you will choose a time commitment that is appropriate to your schedule and development needs. If no time frame is listed, it means there is no minimum requirement. Feel free to increase the time you spend on an activity as you need or want to. You may also find that some activities, such as the KISS or DIRECT processes, may need more frequent practice early in your training but can be performed with less frequency once the concepts they embody become habit.

3. This matrix does not include tools (such as the mission planning tools of Principle 3) because these aren't trained or practiced per se. You will find a complete index of all drills, exercises, and tools at the end of this book for your convenience.

Your Battle Rhythm

Below you will see the daily rhythm of my personal training program, along with those of two of my trainees, Melanie and Jeff. In all three plans, you will notice the rhythm changes for the workweek, where somewhat more regimented training suits the average 9 a.m.–5 p.m. schedule, versus the weekends, which for many Americans are days for family time and relaxation. These are just examples to show you how three people with different needs and obligations arrange their training schedules—you may find that you need to shift everything an hour or two later or earlier, or train more over the weekend rather than during the week, depending on your own work schedule and lifestyle.

Mark's Weekly Training Plan

My total daily training time is slightly more than four hours because of my rigorous physical training schedule (I do two hours of physical workouts every day), but that is a highlight of my day. Then, I use my lunch hour to do more training. For illustrative purposes this schedule seems rigid, but in reality I allow some fluidity. For instance, if I have a particularly busy day at work, I might only do a 20-minute yoga session at lunch. Or I may block off more time to focus on a specific work project. And, throughout the day, I will vary the times and spot practices depending on my schedule and what I need and want to work on.

On weekends, I allow myself to sleep in, and only work if I have a training event or important project. I like to preserve this time for my family. For training I continue my morning practice, and I do a lighter workout on Saturday and what I call "active recovery" on Sunday, which could include surfing, a long run or walk, or a bike ride with my son, Devon.

Monthly, I add the following to my routine: 20X challenge; "checkup from the neck up" therapy session (twice); massage therapy (twice); long run, ruck march (a long hike carrying equipment), or swim (twice); KISS review (once); WOS Assessment check-in (once); date nights (I strive for one weekly, but sometimes travel makes that impossible, so I aim for four per month minimum).

Quarterly, I add the following: one weekend seminar for personal or professional development; quarterly Focus Plan and goals review; one long-weekend getaway with wife or son or both. During my weekends away, I continue to do some type of somatic mind-body training, such as yoga, chi gong, self-defense, or meditation.

Annually, I add the following: one weeklong (or longer) seminar or retreat; annual Focus Plan and goals review; two ten- to fourteen-day vacations with family. During my retreats and vacations, I continue to train but on a modified schedule, depending upon where we are and what I'm doing.

Mark's Weekly Training Plan

Time	Monday	Tuesday	Wednesday
5:30 a.m.	Wake	Wake	Wake
5:30–6:00 a.m.	Morning Ritual	Morning Ritual	Morning Ritual
6:00–6:45 a.m.	Breakfast/Help Devon prep for school	Breakfast/Help Devon prep for school	Breakfast/Help Devon prep for school
7:00–9:00 a.m.	SEALFIT	Take Devon to school/ SEALFIT	SEALFIT Strength (1 hour)/ SEALFIT Self-Defense (1 hour)
9:00 a.m.–12:00 p.m	Work	Work	Work
12:00–1:00 p.m	Yoga (30–45 minutes)/ Lunch	Box Breathing (10 minutes)/Mindful walk (45 minutes)/Lunch	Yoga (30-45 minutes)/ Lunch
1:00–5:00 p.m	Work (focus time for special projects)	Work (focus time for special projects)	Work (focus time for special projects)
5:00–6:00 p.m	Tai chi	Chi gong	Tai chi
6:00–6:15 p.m	Spot practices: Courage Dog check-in & "Future Me" visualization (15 minutes)	Spot practices: Courage Dog check-in & "Future Me" visualization (15 minutes)	Spot practices: Courage Dog check-in & "Future Me" visualization (15 minutes)
7:00–9:00 p.m.	Authentic Communication while having dinner with family	Authentic Communication while having dinner with family	Authentic Communication while having dinner with family
9:00–10:00 p.m.	Reading and time with Sandy	Reading and time with Sandy	Reading and time with Sandy
10:00–10:30 p.m.	Evening Ritual (10 minutes)/Daily Focus Plan (20 minutes)	Evening Ritual (10 minutes)/Daily Focus Plan (20 minutes)	Evening Ritual (10 minutes)/Daily Focus Plan (20 minutes)
10:30 p.m.	Bed	Bed	Bed

Thursday	Friday	Saturday	Sunday
Wake	Wake		
Morning Ritual	Morning Ritual		
Breakfast/Help Devon prep for school	Breakfast/Help Devon prep for school	Morning Ritual	Morning Ritual
SEALFIT	SEALFIT Strength (1 hour)/ SEALFIT Self-Defense (1 hour)	CrossFit	Rest and play with family (all day)
Work	Work		
Box Breathing (10 minutes)/ Mindful walk (45 minutes)/Lunch	Yoga (30-45 minutes)/ Lunch	Authentic Communication while spending time with Devon (most of the day if I am not out of town or at a seminar)	
Work (focus time for special projects)	Work (focus time for special projects)		
Chi gong	SEALFIT team workout		
Spot practices: Courage Dog check-in & "Future Me" visualization (15 minutes)	Spot practices: Courage Dog check-in & "Future Me" visualization (15 minutes)		
Authentic Communication while having dinner with family	Authentic Communication while having dinner with family	Date or social engagement	Authentic Communication while having dinner with family
Reading and time with Sandy	Reading and time with Sandy		
Evening Ritual (10 minutes)/Daily Focus Plan (20 minutes)	Evening Ritual (10 minutes)/Daily Focus Plan (20 minutes)		Evening Ritual (10 minutes)/Weekly Focus Plan (20 minutes)
Bed	Bed		Bed

Melanie's Weekly Training Plan

As a single mom trying to make ends meet, Melanie found herself completely losing track of the most important things in her life—especially her family. She told me that before I met her, she didn't know how to change. "I became resigned to parenting from a place of failure. I felt out of control, exhausted, and scared!" she says of that time of her life. How many single moms are in this same predicament, I wonder? My wife, Sandy, was a single mom for some years before I met her, and the resiliency of this subset of our population amazes me.

Melanie took a parenting class, which gave her some tools to cope. But those were just tips and tricks for managing two young kids (six-year-old Lillian and four-year-old old Drake) more effectively. She felt like there must be another level . . . something much deeper that would lead to a total reorganization of her life and lifestyle for the better. Through my CrossFit gym, Melanie discovered my Unbeatable Mind program. The first lesson focused on calming the mind and creating clarity, a challenge that excited Melanie, who had never meditated a day in her life. After operating on overdrive for so many years, she'd lost the ability to find stillness and calm for even a moment. Now, she was required to practice sacred silence every day, which immediately began to bring peace and focus back into her life.

For Melanie, the second-biggest step toward positive transformation came from the practice of stepping outside of your mental chatter to take a look at the bigger picture (as you do with our DIRECT tool). Soon Melanie found that instead of living on "an emotional roller coaster," just waiting for the next thing to make her laugh, burst into tears, or scream, she could observe her thoughts and emotions with some distance. This moved her from a reactionary state to a mindful state, further calming her and bringing confidence.

Last but not least, her new training program helped Melanie to shift from a deeply negative, fearful mental feedback loop to a place of security and confidence. With no outside help, she had long struggled to make ends meet. Her precarious financial situation left her in constant fear of falling over the edge. Through her positivity practice ("What Dog Are You Feeding?"), she learned to trust herself and even develop optimism about her future. Melanie said to me after a few months of training, "My children are drawn to my new energy and the peace that I am finding. Even though my time with the kids is sometimes limited due to my work, the time I do share is so valuable and precious. I am finally the mom that I always knew I could be!"

Melanie fits in an hour a day of physical training during the workweek, plus another hour and forty-five minutes or so of other WOS practices spread throughout the day. On Wednesdays, she has a neighbor take the kids to school so she can attend a yoga class. She eats breakfast at her desk when she arrives at work and eats lunch after she returns to work from her workout in the afternoons. Some evenings she is running around with the kids, but maintains her spot practices while they are engaged with their activities. Other evenings she is free and will take the kids surfing, or attend a yoga class when the kids are with her mom. Weekends are more flexible and less structured.

Monthly, she adds the following to her routine: do a 20X challenge; learn a new skill in CrossFit; read a book.

Quarterly, she adds the following: one weekend seminar for personal or professional development; one volunteer shift at a homeless shelter; one weekend getaway with the kids.

Annually, she adds the following: one weeklong seminar or retreat; annual Focus Plan and goals review; one weeklong vacation with the kids.

Melanie's Weekly Training Plan

Time	Monday	Tuesday	Wednesday
6:00 a.m.	Wake	Wake	Wake
6:00–6:30 a.m.	Morning Ritual	Morning Ritual	Morning Ritual
6:30–8:00 a.m.	Breakfast/help kids prep for school	Breakfast/help kids prep for school	Yoga (1 hour)
8:00 a.m.–12:00 p.m.	Work	Work	Work
12:00–1:00 p.m.	CrossFit (1 hour)/Lunch	CrossFit (1 hour)/Lunch	CrossFit (1 hour)/Lunch
1:00–4:00 p.m.	Work	Work	Work
4:00–4:10 p.m.	Spot practices: Courage Dog & Breathing (10 minutes)	Spot practices: Courage Dog & Meditation (10 minutes)	Spot practices: Courage Dog & Breathing (10 minutes)
4:10–5:30 p.m.	Work	Work	Work
5:30–7:00 p.m.	Yoga or kids' activity	Surf or kids' activity	Run or kids' activity
7:00–9:00 p.m.	Authentic Communication while having dinner with family	Authentic Communication while having dinner with family	Authentic Communication while having dinner with family
9:30–10:00 p.m.	Evening Ritual	Evening Ritual	Evening Ritual
10:00 p.m.	Bed	Bed	Bed

Jeff's Weekly Training Plan

Jeff discovered SEALFIT and the Unbeatable Mind Academy while working as an expatriate in Europe. His job, a high-stress corporate management position, combined with a crazy travel schedule, left him feeling out of balance. Jeff wanted to improve his overall health and fitness and set himself on a path to business ownership. He also wanted to strengthen his marriage, which suffered from his frequent absenses and unhealthy expressions of stress. Three years later: Jeff is running his own executive coaching business in Zurich, Switzerland, and at age forty-two, he's healthier and fitter than ever. He's patched things up with his wife and they both enjoy more intimacy in their relationship. While a business owner's life is never stress-free,

Thursday	Friday	Saturday	Sunday
Wake	Wake		
Morning Ritual	Morning Ritual		
Breakfast/Help kids prep for school	Breakfast/Help kids prep for school	Morning Ritual (30 minutes)	Morning Ritual (30 minutes)
Work	Work	CrossFit (1 hour)/Rest and play with family (for the rest of the day)	Church (2 hours)/Rest and play with family (for the rest of the day)
Yoga (1 hour)/Lunch	CrossFit (1 hour)/Lunch		
Work	Work		
Spot practices: Courage Dog & Meditation (10 minutes)	Spot practices: Courage Dog & Breathing (10 minutes)		
Work	Work		
Surf or kids' activity	Time with friends		
Authentic Communication while having dinner with family	Authentic Communication while having dinner with family		
Evening Ritual	Evening Ritual	Evening Ritual	
Bed	Bed	Bed	

he reports, "I absolutely address stress now in a much different and certainly healthier manner. I've never been happier, more fulfilled, or more optimistic about the future."

For Jeff, the breathing exercises, visualizations, sacred silence (meditation), and yoga practices were the most surprising aspects of the program and also the most effective: The collective set of practices had a massive impact on his calmness, creativity, and problem-solving. "I wish I had known this stuff all the years I spent locked in marathon negotiation sessions!" he says. As he progressed through his training, he learned how to address his negativity and fears, which included leaving a secure corporate position to found his own company in a foreign country, and how to get more out of his mind, which often seemed too engaged in firefighting to focus on long-term growth and creative entrepreneurship.

The physical component drawn from SEALFIT, while challenging, opened itself to Jeff in stages. As his fitness improved, he reached a level where he felt confident attending Kokoro Camp and taking up a dormant interest in music, which he now performs publicly. The lessons on teamwork, leadership, and thriving in adversity he learned through those experiences, Jeff reports, were never so tangible and vibrantly explained in business school or dozens of leadership books.

Jeff trains and practices for roughly three hours a day during the weekdays. He typically eats lunch at his desk or fuels up as needed throughout the day so he can take an hour for yoga or meditation in the afternoons. Often he will take a short break in the afternoon for a mindful walk or spot practice such as Box Breathing, depending upon

Jeff's Weekly Training Plan

Time	Monday	Tuesday	Wednesday
5:00 a.m.	Wake	Wake	Wake
5:00–5:30 a.m.	Morning Ritual	Morning Ritual	Morning Ritual
6:00–8:00 a.m.	SEALFIT	SEALFIT	SEALFIT
8:00 a.m.–12:00 p.m.	Work	Work	Work
12:00–1:00 p.m.	Yoga (1 hour)/Lunch	Meditation (1 hour)/ Lunch	Yoga (1 hour)/Lunch
1:00–6:00 p.m.	Work	Work	Work
6:00–6:10 p.m.	Spot practices: Courage Dog & Breathing (10 minutes)	Spot practices: Courage Dog & Meditation (10 minutes)	Spot practices: Courage Dog & Breathing (10 minutes)
7:00–9:00 p.m.	Authentic Communication while having dinner with family/Music practice	Authentic Communication while having dinner with family	Authentic Communication while having dinner with family/Music practice
9:00–10:00 p.m.	Reading (50 minutes)/ Evening Ritual (10 minutes)	Reading (50 minutes)/ Evening Ritual (10 minutes)	Reading (50 minutes)/ Evening Ritual (10 minutes)
10:00 p.m.	Bed	Bed	Bed

what he feels he needs. Weekends are more flexible and less intense. Since weekends are prime family time, he often will play an outdoor sport or attend a concert, family get-together, or other cultural event with his wife at that time.

Monthly or quarterly, he adds the following to his routine: do a 20X challenge; learn a new skill in CrossFit or mental development; attend a concert; read two books (one for personal and one for professional development); review Focus Plan and goals; participate in a project with the Big Brother program; date nights (four monthly).

Annually, he adds the following: one weeklong seminar or retreat; annual Focus Plan and goals review; a public performance of his music; one longer service-oriented vacation (typically requiring multiple scheduled events over a period of two months) related to his work with underprivileged youth.

Thursday	Friday	Saturday	Sunday
Wake	Wake		
Morning Ritual	Morning Ritual	Morning Ritual	
SEALFIT	SEALFIT	Long training run	Morning Ritual (30 minutes)
Work	Work	Rest and time with wife (for most of the day)	Yoga (2 hours)/ Rest and time with wife (for most of the day)
Meditation (1 hour)/Lunch	Yoga (1 hour)/Lunch		
Work	Work		
Spot practices: Courage Dog & Meditation (10 minutes)	Spot practices: Courage Dog & Breathing (10 minutes)		
Authentic Communication while having dinner with family	Authentic Communication while having dinner with family/Music practice	Date	
Reading (50 minutes)/ Evening Ritual (10 minutes)	Reading (50 minutes)/ Evening Ritual (10 minutes)	Reading (50 minutes)/ Evening Ritual (10 minutes)	
Bed	Bed	Bed	

Staying the Course

Discipline is the bridge between goals and accomplishment.

—JIM ROHN, AMERICAN ENTREPRENEUR, AUTHOR, AND
MOTIVATIONAL SPEACKER (1930–2009)

As I mentioned previously, it's common for many folks to get side-tracked, lose interest, and settle back into their old ways when the excitement wears off as they enter the "walk" phase. The challenge with whole-person development is that, besides the overt changes brought about through physical training, it's sometimes difficult to note progress in your inner space. This is because inner growth is not linear, like physical growth is—you don't just lift up a barbell and get stronger. Rather, inner growth is nonlinear and exponential. You can go a long time with seemingly no results, then suddenly you have a breakthrough and find yourself with a whole new worldview, level of consciousness, or sense of peace. Here are some recommendations to help you stay the course with your training so that you can reach the point where it will become a habit, then a lifestyle that will continue to fuel your upward spiral of success for life:

- **Set up a permanent space.** It's important to designate a training space at home for your practice sessions, especially your morning and evening rituals, that you can protect from distraction. Once you identify your space, set it up for comfort and with the tools you will need. Over time it will capture the energy of your practice and be an important structural component of your training. Many of my business-leader clients have taken steps to offer a training hall at their work locations for silent time, yoga, and other development activities. This goes a long way toward solidifying their teams' acceptance of the practices and encourages integration.

What about My Kids?

Many parents in my Unbeatable Mind program have reported experiencing breakthroughs with their kids when they shared with them some of the simpler principles in this book. Most, if not all, the WOS practices can be adapted for use with your family or for your kids to use on their own. Among the most powerful for kids are:

- Authentic Communication, for a closer relationship and a deeper understanding that will prove more powerful than any punishments in getting your kids to act in accordance with your values

- "What Dog Are You Feeding?" for maintaining a positive state of mind

- KISS and front-sight focus tools (such as deep breathing cycles and developing a stand) to generate discussions around purpose and values

- Yoga and functional fitness to teach kids how to use their breath for better self-control, develop their physical and mental awareness, and improve flexibility and core strength

For all these reasons and more, I encourage you not to shy away from including your family in your training. It will help you stay focused and on track and introduce them to powerful new ways of approaching life, all while providing a remarkable experience for the whole family. A family that trains together, grows together.

- **Get support.** Sometimes loved ones may feel like the time you spend training is time taken away from them, or they simply may not understand the need to do the practices such as yoga and meditation. These are valid issues and best not shoved under the rug. Bringing your family into the conversation and even your training is a powerful way to build your family team!

- **Stay motivated.** Fatigue or injury, especially as it pertains to physical training, can throw you off course. Making a habit of excellence and forging grit (Principle 5) will help you push through those moments where your progress is frustrated. It's also important to check in with your "why" frequently. I review my purpose daily, which motivates me to keep my training in my front-sight focus.

- **Track your progress.** Some days you just don't feel any different or like you're making any progress. So why are you going to all the trouble? To overcome this obstacle, use your focus plans to benchmark your efforts with carefully chosen microgoals and targets, and commit to a daily journaling practice. As you reflect upon your achievements and how you show up in the world over time, you will gain confidence that the training is working its magic.

- **Refresh your plan.** The newness has worn off . . . now what? Keep showing up and putting in perfect effort, but spice things up with some variety (Principle 6). When you do your quarterly and annual reviews, you can reenergize your training by refreshing your plan. Try a new practice or pursue a new skill, vary your routine schedule, and commit to some new goals.

- **Join practice groups.** You don't have to do this alone. Finding a swim buddy or a practice group can be great for accountability and engaging the power of the team. This has happened spontaneously in our online Unbeatable Mind community and has really helped students stay the course with their training.

The "I" in Team

Standards are not rules issued by the boss; they are a collective
identity. Remember, standards are the things that you do all the
time and the things for which you hold one another accountable.
—MIKE KRZYZEWSKI, USA MEN'S BASKETBALL COACH (1947–)

SEALs are undisputed in the area of team effectiveness. Underneath
the techniques and tactics, our effectiveness stems from the collective
powerhouse of individuals committed to self-mastery, the kind we've
been practicing in this book. But as powerful as each special operator is, we never do anything alone. Have you ever been on a winning
team firing on all cylinders? The synergy among your teammates, the
shared sense of accountability and mission focus was palpable, right?
Everyone was happy, healthy, motivated, and getting things done,
overcoming seemingly insurmountable tasks. Unfortunately, as you
may have guessed, these teams are highly uncommon! If you've experienced an elite team once, you've been lucky. With so many books
written and a billion-dollar training industry focused on team building, why do most teams fall short?

Part of the answer is the lack of commitment to self-mastery
among individuals. However, a winning team is more than just a
collection of individuals operating at an elite level. The individuals
are only one-third of the equation. The team's culture and spirit is
the second third, and the structures and support of the organization
completes the team. Learning how to fully implement the Way of the
SEAL at the team and organizational levels is worthy of a book about
each, and one day I hope to have an opportunity to write them. In
the meantime, I want to talk briefly about the I in your team: How
can you begin effecting change within yours to support your personal
development—and how can your personal development positively affect your team?

You will develop faster in terms of your awareness and sense of self on a team than you would sitting in meditation in Tibet. We all have teams—families, social groups, and work teams—and we spend a lot of our time with them. Let's make that time training time. Whether you are in a leadership position or not, you can introduce many of the principles explored in this book to your team. Breathing exercises, guided visualizations, and planning tools are all great ways to positively affect your team experience. Use meetings as opportunities to test your growing awareness skills. Apply front-sight focus tactics to your next assignment. And, whenever appropriate, model the Way of the SEAL for your team by sharing details of your training and experiences with them—let them see how it's working for you.

When we approach our teams as time to "work on ourselves" while "working in the team" then we, as individuals, contribute to the culture of the team as an elite force. In turn, this elevates our own performance to a higher level in an upward spiral of individual and team success.

Communicate with Brutal Honesty

While many leadership models emphasize communicating a powerful vision and motivating the troops, in reality, listening to them is more effective in gaining their trust. A big shared vision certainly can become a rallying point around which you build your team culture, but remember that each person will interpret the vision differently, based on their individual blind spots and BOO.

The fact that you can't truly share a common experience internally both leads to and is worsened by poor communication, which further exacerbates a lack of understanding, mistrust, and ultimately failed commitments. Therefore, effective communication with brutal honesty is a critical team skill. For a team to develop trust there must be a mandate to listen and communicate and a structure to facilitate these efforts. In the SEALs, the structures we use are the brief and debrief. Let's look more closely at these valuable tools, which each serve different purposes.

The brief, discussed under Principle 2, is done prior to any training or real mission. The brief is a very precise way to convey critical information to the team. It is also when the team gets to ask questions about the mission and their role. Without the brief, mission effectiveness would decrease substantially. You can easily apply all mission-planning and goal-setting tools in this book at a team level.

The debrief occurs after the mission is completed and is the primary mechanism for continuous feedback and course corrections. During the debrief, the team reviews every facet of the mission for information that can lead to improvements in individual behavior or team performance. Also, any issues with the organization's structure that negatively or positively impacted the mission are noted for discussion up the chain of command. The process is simple but not easy to employ because it assumes a high level of trust and accountability already exist in the team. The process is as follows:

1. Debrief as soon as possible after completing a mission. The team leader will usually moderate or you can designate someone else to facilitate. Allow everyone to speak in a round-robin approach—all teammates should be encouraged to find something to say (sometimes the quiet ones have the most interesting contributions).

2. Everything that happened on the mission, whether good, bad, or ugly, is on the table for discussion. This includes personal and team performance, lessons learned, screw-ups as well as breakthroughs, and innovations that occurred spontaneously during the course of the mission. You can either chunk the topics to focus the conversation or just go around the table and see what comes up.

3. Everyone agrees and strives not to take anything personally—egos are checked at the door. What is said in the debrief about personal performance stays in the debrief unless corrective action is required at the

organizational level. New teammates will learn to trust the team on this one as they observe this rule enforced by team leaders as well as all teammates. If the meeting veers off track into a personal attack, the facilitator should employ the "What Dog Are You Feeding?" exercise (or whatever works to bring it back to positive territory for your team) and immediately come back to the facts.

4. Analyze every item for ways to improve at an individual, team, or organizational level. In other words, the debrief is not a bitch session. Time is spent very judiciously with an eye toward continuous refinement of the team's winning culture.

5. Note action items and follow up on them by making changes in individual training plans or operational, administrative, or logistics processes.

The team debrief was one of the key tools I introduced to the U.S. women's cycling team in their run-up to the 2012 London Olympics. When they brought me in as a consultant, they were having trouble communicating with their coaching staff and had trust issues internally; they had never worked together for more than a couple of weeks at a time and were now together daily for more than two and a half months. As individuals, they were accustomed to being top performers, but as a team, they were five long seconds out of the running for a medal.

First, I encouraged the most experienced athlete in the group, Jennie Reed, to assume a leadership role in communicating honestly and directly with the coaching staff. In addition, we created a moment after every training session to debrief—first, just amongst the athletes themselves; and then with their coaches involved. "Rather than feel powerless," Jennie told the team, "let's sit down and envision what we need as a team to make the training work for us and make up those five seconds!" She asked her teammates to write out a revised training program to present to the coaching staff.

Soon, the conversations in their debriefs transformed from "The coaches are making us do this and it's not working!" to "We're doing exactly what we believe in our hearts will make up the time and bring a medal within reach." They learned not to fear breakdowns and conflict happening at the right times—they didn't deny or ignore their very real fears of failure and uncertainty; rather, they worked with the positive energy of "can do, if we do it together."

By the time they traveled to London for the Olympic Games, the underdog team had a level of confidence previously unknown to the group. They shocked the world (and themselves) by beating heavily favored Australia in the semifinal and went on to win a silver medal against Great Britain. Afterward, they told me, "What we learned is that you don't need an institution, tradition, or doping to create exceptional performances. With the right attention to the right things, it's possible to have breakthroughs like this." Their stunning performance was later profiled in the documentary *Personal Gold*.

For the brief and debrief to work well, teammates must be good listeners. I highly recommend practicing the Authentic Communication exercise from Principle 7's Exercises section at a team level as part of the debrief process. This will help you quiet the critical voice in your head so you can better tune in to what your teammate is saying, and your teammates will learn to do the same—you will learn to truly listen to one another and, perhaps most important of all, to truly hear one another.

LEAD WITH YOUR HEART

It matters not how strait the gate,
How charged with punishments the scroll,
I am the master of my fate:
I am the captain of my soul.
—WILLIAM ERNEST HENLEY, BRITISH POET AND CRITIC
(1849–1903)

When you embark on the path to developing self-mastery, you are committing to truth, and then to developing wisdom, and then to leading with heart. While truth is found through refinement of intellect, wisdom and heart are found through moral courage. Risking loss and failure forges moral courage—bringing the challenge to you allows you to meet your true self. Though I have leaned into challenge and struggled with loss and failure in my life, I have grown immeasurably from both. Now it is your time to step up.

The type of global paradigm change we face, the work required to steer the ship in a new direction, is too overwhelming to expect any single political, spiritual, academic, or warrior leader to rise up and lead us through the mess. No, it must be an individual, team, and systemic level effort where we all unite for an upwelling of honor, courage, and commitment. This time it is not just for your home team, but for THE home team of our human race. What inspiration can I offer to guide you as you move forward? How about a WOS stand?

1. I know why I am doing what I am doing. I will not allow the winds of pain or pleasure to blow me off course from my stand, nor will I let the desires of others distract me from my purpose. I embrace risk, loss, and failure as necessary companions and teachers on my journey.

2. I will win in my mind before seeking to win in the arena. I am committed to self-mastery.

3. When faced with challenges, I embrace the suck, get the job done, and keep moving on to the next task. I know I am capable of 20 times more than I think I am.

4. I display integrity and authenticity in thought, word, and deed—alone, with teammates, and within the "systems" defining my life.

5. I never shy from hard leadership roles, yet I step back when it is someone else's turn. I am not after power, glory, money, or fame—rather, the experience to lead and serve on my journey to self-mastery.

6. I am driven by my passions and my purpose, not a need for titles or accolades.

7. I go to the challenge and strive for self-control, desiring to forge my mental toughness so I can earn a Trident of respect every day.

8. I never quit in training or on an "op," and I never leave a teammate behind.

9. I acknowledge and am open to my inner wisdom, ever seeking to expand my awareness; eradicate faulty thinking; and cultivate a strong mind, body, and spirit connection.

10. I strive to remain innovative, creative, and offense-oriented in my approach to all things. I don't fear failure and I never shy from risk. I am always learning and growing.

11. I train realistically and aggressively, coming back to basics often. I take nothing for granted and work tirelessly to hone my skills for extraordinary results.

One day not too long ago, Glen Doherty and I were finishing a conversation about training at SEALFIT HQ. A former SEAL and one of my top staff coaches, Glen was passionate about our programs, but he earned his real living as a hired contractor for the CIA.

"When do you head back to the playground, Glen?" I asked.

"I'm out the door on Wednesday," he said. "I'm hoping this will be my last gig."

"Really? That would be great!" My voice revealed hope that Glen would hang up this line of work soon. After twenty years serving as a SEAL and "other agency" contractor, he had already given and risked so much. He had a huge heart and lived every bit of the WOS stand I just outlined, but I was worried about him.

"Yeah, I'm getting tired of this shit. I want to settle down and dig into something new," Glen said.

It was the last time I saw him. I got the text from our mutual friend Brandon Webb, author of *The Red Circle*, on September 12, 2012. "Bad news, Glen was killed in Libya" was all it said. I had heard about the uproar in Benghazi about the supposed video that bashed Islam, but a mob overrunning the embassy surprised me. The U.S. is usually good about securing its diplomatic outposts. My team and I were devastated about the news and sought to learn more.

What I learned was that on that fateful day, Glen, as I would have expected, upheld the code of the warrior and reinforced the courage ethos for us all. Though details are still emerging as of this writing, Glen and his teammate Ty Woods, also a former SEAL, heard the sound of gunfire as they sat in their safe house in Benghazi. On their radio, they also heard calls for help from the embassy staff, and I imagine they took about one second to think about it before advising their station chief of their plans and jumping into their vehicle. Grabbing weapons from the fleeing Libyan security guards, Glen and Ty fought their way into the embassy and freed eighteen Americans. When the embassy was finally secured after a four-hour gunfight, they returned to their safe house. Unfortunately, they were followed by the militant operators who had overtaken the embassy—and at a hundred-to-one odds, these warriors fought with the hearts of lions for another ten hours until a mortar ended their last stand.

Glen is an inspiration, and his spirit infuses this book. The full story of Benghazi is yet to be told. But Glen and other authentic warriors like him teach us how important it is to lead with heart, to risk it all to do the right thing. Death may not be a risk for you, but if you enact each day as if your life depended on it, if you prepare for those moments of performance by making a habit of excellence and living in alignment with the highest standards, you can tap into the same extraordinary results that generations of heroes have before you.

Let the sacrifice of these warriors be our wake-up call—let's honor them and ourselves and step up. Hooyah!

Appendix 1:
Focus Plans

Checking in with your focus plans regularly will lead you to take powerful KISS actions every day. You won't waste time on anything that doesn't move you toward your goals. When you get superfocused every day, week, month/quarter, and year on those top two or three things that are connected to your passion, purpose, and mission, your thoughts and actions naturally align. When you're in alignment, it's easier to stack up victories, which develops confidence, which in turn supports your simplifying efforts, and so on in an upward cycle of success!

Photocopy these worksheets as many times as you need. With each one, don't forget to fill in the appropriate date, month, quarter, or year.

Daily/Weekly Focus Plan for _____

The One Thing (the most important thing I will achieve this day and/or week):

_____

_____

_____

Priority Tasks (that I must complete today or this week): _____

_____

_____

_____

Projects (to work on one step at a minimum each day): _____

_____

_____

_____

Contacts (calls/e-mails to people I need to connect with): _____

_____

_____

_____

Habit (what am I working on this week, and how): _____

_____

_____

_____

Notes, Ideas, and Inspirations (any ideas that came up during the morning ritual found in Appendix 2): _____

_____

_____

_____

_____

_____

_____

_____

_____

_____

_____

_____

_____

Quarterly Focus Plan for _____

The One Thing (the most important thing I will achieve this quarter):

_____

_____

_____

_____

Top 3 Targets for the Quarter: _____

_____

_____

_____

_____

_____

Top 3 Tasks for Each Target: _____

_____

_____

_____

_____

_____

_____

Top Contacts to Make: _____

_____

_____

_____

_____

_____

New Habit to Integrate: _____

_____

_____

_____

_____

_____

_____

_____

Notes, New Ideas, and Inspirations: _____

_____

_____

_____

_____

_____

_____

_____

_____

_____

_____

_____

_____

_____

_____

_____

_____

_____

_____

Annual Focus Plan for _____

Purpose/Vision for My Life (carry forward and adjust as it evolves):

_____

_____

Vision for my Business or Work Role (carry forward and adjust as it evolves):

_____

_____

_____

Top 6 Values (and what I can do this year to get closer to them): _____

_____

_____

_____

_____

_____

Top 3 Mission Goals for My Life (carry forward and adjust as they evolve):

_____

_____

_____

_____

Top 3 Mission Goals for the Next 3 Years (carry forward and adjust as they evolve):

_____

_____

_____

_____

Top 3 Targets for This Year: _____

_____

_____

Must-Dos for Reaching My Top 3 Targets: _____

_____

_____

_____

_____

Top 20 Contacts to make: _____

_____

_____

_____

_____

_____

_____

New Habit to Integrate: _____

_____

_____

_____

_____

_____

_____

Notes, Ideas, and Inspirations (have/be/do list): _____

_____

_____

_____

_____

_____

_____

Appendix 2:
Power Rituals

Performing these Power Rituals daily and as needed (they could be adjusted slightly for use just before or after an important event, respectively) helps train your mind to start and end each day and each important challenge in a positive, powerful "performance zone" state.

The Morning Ritual

When you awake in the morning, the first thing you will do is drink a large glass of fresh water, and then sit comfortably with your journal in a quiet space—preferably one dedicated to your reflective and visualization work—and ask yourself the following empowering questions. Write down whatever comes up.

- What and whom am I grateful for today?
- What am I excited about and looking forward to doing today?
- What is my purpose, and do my plans for today connect me to it?
- How can I move the dial toward my goals today?
- To whom can I reach out and serve or thank today?
- Are my goals still aligned with my purpose?

Next, spend a minimum of five minutes Box Breathing, then spend a minimum of five minutes in mindful movement (I do up to an hour some days). My preference is yoga, but tai chi, chi gong, or a short mindful walk will work. Finally, before you start your day, review your Daily Focus Plan. Make any adjustments to ensure it's in alignment with the answers to your morning questions, and block time in your schedule for key project work or training.

The Evening Ritual

Before you settle in for the night, sit comfortably with your journal in a quiet space—preferably one dedicated to your reflective and visualization work—and ask yourself the following empowering questions. Write down whatever comes up.

- Was I "on" and in the zone today or "off" and unbalanced?
- What contributed to this feeling?
- What were the top three positive things I accomplished or that happened today? What did I learn from them?
- Are there unsolved challenges I would like my subconscious mind to help me solve tonight?
- What went wrong today and what is the silver lining?

Now enter a meditative state using deep or Box Breathing, and then enter your mind gym in order to review your major goals and continue your ongoing visualization work. While in your mind gym, put any questions or problems that are bugging you to your counselor or to your subconscious. Pay attention to your dreams and any waking thoughts the next day—the answer will usually be there for you.

Pre-Event Ritual

Use this ritual when facing a major mission, race, or challenge and you simply must be at your peak. Once habituated, this can be a five-minute exercise with a powerful impact on your performance.

First, as you approach the time of the event (depending upon the duration and difficulty of the event, this can be days, hours, or minutes before go-time), take action to avoid external distractions (some events, like a race or workout, have a known start time; others are not as known, but this principle applies in either situation). So find a quiet space where you can be alone, perhaps sitting in the car or in a separate room. If you are in a crowded area, just sit and close your eyes and people will leave you alone. Don't worry about what others think about you—they're likely jealous that you have the courage to take care of yourself instead of engaging in the common nervous pre-event chit-chat.

Next, perform a "dirt-dive" visualization to size up your performance in the event and size down your enemy. The enemy can be an actual opponent, other competitors, or even your board of directors! In this visualization, see yourself dominating the situation, totally in control, and see your competitor as capitulating, congratulating you, or weak and ineffective—whatever is appropriate for your situation. Basically you want to see yourself as powerful and crushing the challenge and your opposition as weak and easily overcome. It's important to do both parts of this visualization because we tend to give our opponents or challenges more power than they deserve—we need to cut them down to size and build ourselves up. Focus on your physiology and psychology during each stage of the event as you see it unfold in your mind. Perform deep breathing during this dirt dive. This sets the stage for the rest of the ritual.

Next review your goals and strategy for the mission or challenge. See yourself accomplishing these with ease. Double-check your strategy against the reality of the moment: Is it KISS? Are there any last-minute modifications you need to make? Is there a way to make it even simpler? Are you prepared for the unknown with contingency plans?

Finally, initiate an internal dialogue with a powerful mantra to maintain a positive mind-set, speech, posture, and state of being as you finish your pre-event ritual and launch into performing.

Postevent Ritual

Begin with the "What's the Silver Lining?" exercise on page 132. When you've completed that, you'll want to redirect your attention to a new mission or challenge, and reengage your planning and training. This will be an iterative process, but it can be started in this postevent ritual with some ideas jotted down about what's next. When I competed in the CrossFit Games Open, I had to think carefully about whether to do it again—the time commitment to train for the unique skills is intense and took me off-course a bit from the core SEALFIT physical training model. This postevent course correction can reveal a lot of interesting things. What if you voluntarily took a challenge like an Iron Man race, but you really did not enjoy the process or the event? Would you do another Iron Man just because you can? I wouldn't waste major chunks of life training for something I didn't enjoy the first time! What is another goal or 20X challenge you can set instead?

For a business venture, it may be that your first shot was off the mark. Would you try the same thing again, and if so, how would you adjust your approach? Most entrepreneurial ventures take three or more shots to find the product or revenue model that gets the gears to click. Reframing, reflecting, and redirecting your efforts will help you stay on purpose and moving on the right goals. Ensure that in this process you also reconnect with your "why" and get squarely behind the new goal to reenergize yourself so you can hit it hard when you get back to the playing field the next day.

Appendix 3:
The Way of the SEAL Reading List

What follows is a list of books I have found helpful to me on my journey, and that I think you will enjoy as well. They appear in no particular order other than by category, as noted.

Success and Leadership Philosophy

Unbeatable Mind by Mark Divine
A Theory of Everything by Ken Wilber
Man's Search for Meaning by Viktor Frankl
Think and Grow Rich by Napoleon Hill
The Law of Success by Napoleon Hill
Awaken the Giant Within by Anthony Robbins
Being Peace by Thich Nhat Hanh
The Yoga Sutras by Patanjali
As a Man Thinketh by James Allen
The Silva Mind Control Method by José Silva
The Power of Now by Eckhart Tolle
Grandfather by Tom Brown Jr.
The 4-Hour Workweek by Timothy Ferriss
The Talent Code by Daniel Coyle
The Soul of Leadership by Deepak Chopra
Leadership and Self-Deception by the Arbinger Institute
In Search of the Warrior Spirit by Richard Strozzi-Heckler
Unleash the Warrior Within by Richard J. Machowicz
Thoughts of a Philosophical Fighter Pilot by James B. Stockdale

On Killing by Lieutenant Colonel Dave Grossman
Book of Five Rings by Myomato Musashi
The Art of War by Sun Tzu
The War of Art by Steven Pressfield
Ageless Body Timeless Mind by Deepak Chopra
The Answer to How Is Yes by Peter Block
The Present by Spencer Johnson
An Invented Life by Warren Bennis
Jacob the Baker by Noah benShea
7 Habits of Highly Effective People by Stephen R. Covey
The Story of Philosophy by Will Durant
Thinking, Fast and Slow by Daniel Kahneman
Flow by Mihaly Csikszentmihalyi
Abundance by Peter Diamandis and Steven Kotler

Kokoro and Warrior Spirit

The Fighter's Mind by Sam Sheridan
Mind Power by Kazumi Tabata
Karate-Do: My Way of Life by Gichin Funakoshi
One Day One Lifetime by Tadashi Nakamura
The Warrior Ethos by Steven Pressfield
Born to Run by Christopher McDougall
There Is a Spiritual Solution to Every Problem by Wayne W. Dyer
Light on Yoga by B. K. S. Iyengar
Light on Pranayama by B. K. S. Iyengar
Zen Mind, Beginner's Mind by Shunryu Suzuki
Three Pillars of Zen by Philip Kapleau
Awakening Spirits by Tom Brown
The Intuitive Warrior by Michael Jaco
Warrior Mindset by Michael Asken
Living the Martial Way by Forrest E. Morgan
Essential Spirituality by Roger Walsh
Gates of Fire by Steven Pressfield

Unbroken by Laura Hillenbrand
The Long Walk by Slavomir Rawicz
Extreme Fear by Jeff Wise
Spec Ops: Case Studies by Admiral William McRaven
The Warrior Elite by Dick Couch
You Want Me to Do What? by Jeff Kraus
The Heart and the Fist by Eric Greitens

Fitness and Nutrition

8 Weeks to SEALFIT by Mark Divine
CrossFit Journal articles "What Is Fitness?" and "What Is CrossFit?"
    by Greg Glassman
Starting Strength by Mark Rippetoe
Natural Hormonal Enhancement by Rob Faigin
The Paleo Solution by Robb Wolf
Fixing Your Feet, Fourth Edition by John Vonhof

Index of Tools, Drills, and Exercises

About the Authors

A native of Oneida County, New York, **Mark Divine** served in the U.S. Navy SEALs for 20 years, retiring as a commander. As the founder of SEALFIT, NavySEALs.com, and U.S. CrossFit, he has coached thousands of Navy SEAL and other Special Ops candidates to succeed in the most demanding military training programs in the world, with a success rate near 90 percent.

In his new Unbeatable Mind Academy (unbeatablemind.com), Mark trains the public in the eight Way of the SEAL principles. This integral leadership program combines Western and Eastern practices into the most effective training program in the world for warriors, athletes, professionals, and leaders from all walks of life.

An MBA from New York University's Leonard N. Stern Business School, Mark has run six multimillion dollar business ventures. He also holds several black belts and teaches CrossFit, yoga, and self-defense. The author of *8 Weeks to SEALFIT* and *Unbeatable Mind,* he lives with his wife, Sandy, and son, Devon, in Encinitas, California, where they can be found training and growing with their team.

Allyson Edelhertz Machate (allymachate.com) is a Phi Beta Kappa member and the founder of Ambitious Enterprises, an award-winning business that offers expert writing and editorial services to business professionals, publishers, agents, and authors. A New York native, she leads a team of content professionals from her home near Baltimore, Maryland.